ESSENTIAL PSYCHOLOGY
General Editor
Peter Herriot

F1

NEED TO CHANGE?

GW00746671

ESSENTIAL

PSYCHOLOGY

NEED TO CHANGE?

Fay Fransella

Methuen

First published 1975 by Methuen & Co Ltd
11 New Fetter Lane, London EC4P 4EE
© 1975 Fay Fransella
Printed in Great Britain by
Richard Clay (The Chaucer Press), Ltd
Bungay, Suffolk

ISBN (hardback) 0 416 82170 7
ISBN (paperback) 0 416 82180 4

We are grateful to Grant McIntyre
of Open Books Publishing Ltd for assistance
in the preparation of this series

Contents

Acknowledgements

This book would not have met the publisher's dead-line (which really *was* a dead-line) unless my husband had thought it natural to undertake 'woman's work' while I pounded a typewriter over seemingly endless weekends. Next, I wish to thank Susan Sainsbury and Jaqueline Tyers for typing again and yet again the results of these original weekend poundings. Lastly, to Derek Bolton my gratitude for acting as unofficial philosophy adviser; his constructive criticisms were invaluable and any inaccuracies that remain are entirely my responsibility.

Editor's
Introduction

Fay Fransella shows how our views of science are derived from philosophical theories which are historically rooted in Western thought. She suggests that we should conceive of man as subject, rather than object, actively construing his environment. Then she indicates how such a change of emphasis would affect the ways in which we currently behave towards those who have problems.

Need to Change? belongs to Unit F of *Essential Psychology*. What unifies the books in this unit is the concept of change, not only in people but also in psychology. Both the theory and the practice of the subject are changing fast. The assumptions underlying the different theoretical frameworks are being revealed and questioned. New basic assumptions are being advocated, and consequently new frameworks constructed. One example is the theoretical framework of 'mental illness': the assumptions of normality and abnormality are being questioned, together with the notions of 'the cause', 'the cure', and 'the doctor-patient relationship'. As a result, different frameworks are developing, and different professional practices gradually being initiated. There are, though, various social and political structures which tend to inhibit the translation of changing theory into changing practice.

One interesting change is the current aversion to theoretical frameworks which liken human beings to something else. For example, among many psychologists the analogy of the human being as a computer which characterizes Unit A is in less favour than the concepts of development (Unit C) and the person (Unit D).

Essential Psychology as a whole is designed to reflect this changing structure and function of psychology. The authors are both academics and professionals, and their aim has been to introduce the most important concepts in their areas to beginning students. They have tried to do so clearly, but have not attempted to conceal the fact that concepts that now appear central to their work may soon be peripheral. In other words, they have presented psychology as a developing set of views of man, not as a body of received truth. Readers are not intended to study the whole series in order to 'master the basics'. Rather, since different people may wish to use different theoretical frameworks for their own purposes, the series has been designed so that each title stands on its own. But it is possible that if the reader has read no psychology before, he will enjoy individual books more if he has read the introductions (A1, B1 etc.) to the units to which they belong. Readers of the units concerned with applications of psychology (E, F) may benefit from reading all the introductions.

A word about references in the text to the work of other writers – e.g. 'Smith (1974)'. These occur where the author feels he must acknowledge an important concept or some crucial evidence by name. The book or article referred to will be listed in the bibliography (which doubles as name index) at the back of the book. The reader is invited to consult these sources if he wishes to explore topics further.

We hope you enjoy psychology.

Peter Herriot

I
Changes in man's conception of himself

I The common path

It may seem strange to start off a book that is going to introduce seven other books on the subject of psychology, society and change by talking of people such as Plato, Aristotle, and Galileo. Even more surprising when several of the books in this unit will contain passionate pleas for change in the thinking of psychologists. But who is to say where change begins? Each change must surely be in relation to something in the past. It may therefore be useful to climb down this ladder of change to see how past thinking has led to present action.

Aristotle's view in the mid third century BC was new in certain respects from what had gone before. And one of the things that had gone before was Socrates' method of dialectical reasoning. Socrates lived between 469 BC and 399 BC. He had no particular system of philosophy to hand down (indeed he never admitted to having any knowledge to impart) but he described a method for seeking 'truth'. This method basically involved the asking of questions. During the ensuing discussion, with the argument ranging between the point in question and its opposite, truth would result.

But it was Plato (427 BC to 347 BC) who made Socrates

famous by writing the dialogues in which Socrates was the central figure. And Plato did have a system of philosophy. For him, man had a body and, far and away more important, a soul. All souls existed previously in a world of Being, which was perfect and unchanging, and of which the natural world is but a pale reflection. At birth the soul enters the body, leaving the perfect world, and becoming part of nature.

Man thus has innate knowledge which he brings with him at birth, but which he 'forgets'. It is by dialectical reasoning, by seeking contradictions, that man has a chance of gaining some new knowledge or some glimpse of this 'forgotten' truth. Man thus need not look outside himself for knowledge. He *can* obtain hypotheses from the senses but these would be transformed into ideas which, in turn, would form the basis for the ding-dong question and answer dialectic discussion.

But from the psychologist's point of view, Aristotle was the man who laid down many of the ground rules for much of modern psychology. Aristotle was a logician and a biologist who lived between 384 BC and 322 BC. He argued against the dialectic method of seeking truth, saying that knowledge does not come from the intellect alone for one comes to know things through the senses – by the observation of events:

Lack of experience diminishes our power of taking a comprehensive view of the admitted facts. Hence, those who dwell in intimate association with nature and its phenomena grow more and more able to formulate, as the foundation of their theories, principles such as to admit of a wide and coherent development; while those whom devotion to abstract discussion rendered unobservant of the facts are too ready to dogmatize on the basis of a few observations. (Aristotle, 1952:262)

Aristotelian man is a 'natural', rational animal. He is a part of nature and can play his own part within nature (See F7 in

10

Essential Psychology). One of the features of this man-animal is that he can reason. But knowledge is part of the natural world – it is not innate – truth cannot come simply from the intellect, it must come via the senses as well. Aristotle was not arguing that man could *not* reason dialectically but was arguing that this was of secondary importance to reasoning *demonstratively*. One of his reasons for rejecting the dialectic as a method for seeking philosophic truths was that there was no guarantee that truth could come out of error. You could start with an error and finish with an error. Thus, whereas for Plato reason was far more important than experience, for Aristotle both were necessary.

In addition to formulating the principle of demonstrative reasoning (which is related to our present-day concern with empirical research), Aristotle gave us the idea of the four 'causes'. By pointing to the cause of things, one is bound to adopt the demonstrative rather than the dialectical line of reasoning. The *material* cause simply describes the material from which an object is made: 'I know this is a book because, like most books, it is made of paper and not of wood or stone or chewing gum.' The *formal* cause concerns the form or pattern or outline that books normally have: it 'looks like' a book. The *efficient* cause is the act of setting the type, cutting the pages and putting the book together. The *final* cause is 'that for the sake of which' the book comes into being – its reason for existence.

Our next step on the ladder of change is somewhat crowded containing as it does, amongst many others, Galileo, Descartes, Hobbes, and Locke. But this was the seventeenth century – the peak of the Renaissance and, later, the beginning of the Enlightenment. Here one sees the beginnings of the great upsurge of modern science and philosophy, and the gradual decline of theology.

Galileo, who was born in 1564, proceeded to link thought or theory with fact and practical experiment. It was he who brought mathematics into scientific research, arguing that we could not hope to know the nature of things without a knowledge of mathematics:

> Philosophy is written in that great book which ever lies before our eyes – I mean the universe – but we cannot understand it if we do not first learn the language and grasp the symbols, in which it is written. This book is written in the mathematical language, and the symbols are triangles, circles and other geometrical figures, without whose help it is impossible to comprehend a single word of it; without which one wanders in vain through a dark labyrinth. (Burtt, 1955:75)

Galileo's opinion was that by doing a number of experiments one could generalize and make inferences far beyond the 'fact' discovered: 'the knowledge of a single fact acquired through a discovery of its causes prepares the mind to understand and ascertain other facts without need or recourse to experiment'. (1955:76) He did not think the experiment was the be-all and end-all of scientific inquiry. You only experimented when your thinking or reasoning led you to two alternative conclusions. An experiment was a question put to nature, thus implying some communication between yourself and the world.

Descartes (1586–1650) made explicit what Galileo had implied. He said that man's body is mechanical but that the mind is its own master and *distinct* from the body. A great deal of human behaviour can be explained in terms of natural physiological laws, but certain behaviours cannot be so described: 'two different principles of our movement are to be distinguished – the one entirely mechanical or corporeal, which depends solely on the force of the animal spirits and the configuration of our bodily parts ... the other, incorporeal, that is to say mind or soul which we may define as a substance which thinks'. (1649:358) For Descartes the body and mind interact so that actions are effects produced in the body by the mind, and sensations, emotions and so forth are effects produced in the mind by the body.

It was Isaac Newton (1642–1727) who developed Galileo's scientific method into the form that is recognizable today. He was so successful with his new procedure that it became possible to see science as a passive (observational) way of understanding the world. There were no longer any final causes in nature – there were no intentions, no goals. Scientists must explain things only in terms of efficient and material causes.

Newton also extended Galileo's ideas about the world so that they encompassed the planets as well as the world – they were of the same kind. Newton saw the entire cosmos as functioning like a perfect machine, and there were precise laws that governed its movements which the scientist could discover by experiment. Having observed an event it is possible to discover what has caused that event. Man's body is part of nature and so all his 'events' have discoverable 'causes'. Thus the image of a truly passive man, an acted-upon machine, was well on its way.

But prior to this, Descartes was having an argument with Hobbes (1588–1679). Hobbes was saying that Descartes' notion of dualism was wrong. Man is *only* a mechanical body; he is *only* matter; he has no mind distinct from the body. It is because of his view that man is just a material body that Hobbes is seen as the 'standard' materialist. In addition to having this view of man, Hobbes attempted to apply Galileo's principles of measurement to the study of man, just as it had been applied in the study of physics. He believed that truth is to be found 'out there' and can only be gleaned through the senses and hence by observation. There was now no room for reasoning as a basis for understanding, understanding comes passively.

But, perhaps luckily for man, Locke did not entirely agree with Hobbes. Locke (1632–1704) did agree with Hobbes that man is best seen in mechanical terms (all behaviour and thought are caused rather than being spontaneous), but he disagreed that man was nothing more than a body. Locke accepted Descartes' dualism. He thought that man has a mind as well as a body but believed that the mind works, like the body, on mechanical principles – mental mechanics as opposed to material mechanics. Man for Locke is essentially a passive creature with a mind that is a *tabula rasa*, a blank sheet, on which external events imprint themselves through the senses. This is the defining characteristic of *empiricism*.

The principles on which the mind operates after having 'received' these sensory impressions is described in terms of association. It was Locke's view that the study of these association principles of the mind (that is, the mind's mental 'mechanics') should form the subject matter of psychology. These laws of association were later elaborated by Hume (1711–1776), and Hume's elaborations led, in their turn, to the school of *introspectionists*.

The *introspectionists* tried to study the mechanics of the mind by self-observation. Introspection was a kind of looking at oneself from the inside, as if one were an object to be studied. The belief was that the only access to the mind is through the study of each individual by himself. Introspectionism was a method rather than a theoretical position and is of great importance since it was the rejection of this introspective principle that heralded the rise of behaviourism.

II A parting of the ways

The empiricists gave us a model of man whose mind was passive – a *tabula rasa* – onto which things picked up by our senses were imprinted. For the Würzburg group of introspectionists the mind was also passive, working as it did on the principle of mental mechanics. The method of introspection, of turning one's attention inward and, in so doing, analysing the content of the mind, was a dismal failure as the basis for an experimental procedure for the study of the mind (See A1 in *Essential Psychology*). But it did influence another theorist who developed a method of introspection still very widely used today. This theorist's name was Sigmund Freud.

a) On the path to the ping-pong ball model of man

At first sight it seems a bit unfair to put Freud in this category for, after all, he proposed a dynamic theory of personality (see D3). There is an energy, a psychic energy, that is responsible for human behaviour. This energy resides in the basic structure of the personality – the *id*. In time the person develops an impression of the self, and of a separation between this self and the environment, which constitutes the *ego*. The third part of the personality, and the last to develop, is the *superego*. This superego develops out of the ego as the child takes over the parent's standards and applies them to himself.

The id, as the reservoir of psychic energy, becomes synonymous with the unconscious. Our unconscious wishes, desires, and conflicts, seek outlets and sometimes succeed, as evidenced by our seemingly irrational or guilt-provoking behaviour. By a form of introspection called *free association* (which forms the basis of psychoanalysis as a therapeutic procedure), Freud thought it possible to plumb the depths of the unconscious and find 'truth'.

In Freudian theory, man is again viewed as passive, in the sense that the dynamic aspect of the mind is unconscious. The mind is thus not under the control of reason but under the control of unconscious mechanics.

Bannister (1966) gives a graphic account (although more descriptive of nineteenth rather than twentieth century psychoanalytic theory) of the dynamic model man. 'He is essentially a battlefield, a dark cellar in which a maiden aunt and a sex-crazed monkey are locked in mortal combat, the affair being refereed by a rather nervous bank clerk.' (1966: 363)

Whereas Freud built upon the introspectionists' method in the formulation of his own theory of personality, J. B. Watson found the whole introspectionist school totally unacceptable:

Psychology as the behaviourist views it is a purely objective experimental branch of natural science. Its theoretical goal is the prediction and control of behaviour. Introspection forms no essential part of its methods, nor is the scientific value of its data dependent upon the readiness with which they lend themselves to interpretation in terms of consciousness. The behaviourist, in his efforts to get a unitary scheme of animal response, recognizes no dividing line between man and brute. (1913:158)

The whole emphasis of psychological inquiry was now to focus on learning – on showing how stimulus-response connections (associations) could be strengthened and new ones established (see A3). All subjective matter was thrown out of the window and objectivism became the order of the day. The only data that were to be considered 'proper' were those obtained by independent observers at the same event.

The denying of concepts of consciousness and mind as legitimate areas of investigation in human beings (see F7 for a discussion of their return) resulted in the study of a mindless object that responded blindly to stimuli in the environment. Having dehumanized man, it was not really surprising that for many years to come psychologists considered the most suitable organism for study to be the animal rather than the human. This led in time to the amassing of a considerable body of data on the prison behaviour of the rat.

Watson had nothing that could be called a theory about the psychological functioning of the human or the rat. What he did have was a revolutionary alternative method to the existing subjective method focused on introspection. But he quickly found something on which to latch his alternative view – and that was the work of Pavlov (see A3). By 1924, all the problems of learning were couched in terms of 'conditioning' by Watson. Koch gives an interesting account of how this holy alliance came about:

Watson spent much of the summer of 1916 in a frantic effort to obtain photographic records of implicit speech movements. The hope was to present such pictures of the physical basis of thinking in his presidential address to the American Psychological Association which he was to give that fall. But about two weeks before the scheduled time for the address, it became apparent that success was not likely to be forthcoming. Watson rapidly shifted tack. Lashley, then a student in his laboratory, had been doing work on human salivary and motor conditioning. For his address, Watson hurriedly wrote up on this research, along with vigorous recommendation of the use of conditioning methods (then but slightly known outside of Russia). (Koch, 1964:9)

By such quirks of fate the die was cast that directed the work of psychology for many decades.

The problem for behaviour theory became the problem of explaining how and why organisms react to stimuli in their environment but it was left to Hull in the 1930s to evolve a systematic theory of learning. Hull's theory, like Watson's original approach, was mechanistic and explicitly avoids any reference to such unscientific notions as consciousness, but Hull took behaviourism many steps further. He developed a precise theoretical system based on Pavlov's conditioning principles but also sought to explain such things as purposes and insights. For Hull, the unit or central concept to study was the *habit* (the association between stimulus (S) and response (R), usually expressed as sH_R), along with the concept of *drive* (see D2).

Since man never acts, but only reacts, there had to be some explanation of why he ever gets started at all. Thus the ubiquitous notion of drive was used to explain the activation of behaviour and the notion of drive reduction was evoked to explain the reinforcement or strengthening of S–R connections (see D2).

Hull and his contemporaries did not go to the physical sciences for support for their arguments, but to philosophers and they latched on to logical positivism for a model of science. The logical positivists were members of a philosophical school of thought and included such people as A. J. Ayer and R. Carnap. The *principle of verification* was the main idea that Hull borrowed from these people. In its strong form the principle is stated by Ayer as follows:

The criterion which we use to test the genuineness of apparent statements of fact is the criterion of verifiability. We say that a sentence is factually significant to any given person, if, and only if, he knows how to verify the proposition which it purports to express – that is, if he knows what observations would lead him, under certain conditions, to accept the proposition as being true, or reject it as being false.... We enquire in every case what observations would lead us to answer the question, one way or the other; and, if none can be discovered, we must conclude that the sentence under consideration does not, as far as we are concerned, express a genuine question, however strongly its grammatical appearance may suggest that it does. (Ayer, 1946:35)

This meant, for example, that all scientific propositions were equivalent to sets of propositions describing experimental observations.

But Carnap discovered that this was false. There was no *translation* of, for example, 'water is made of H_2 and O' into experiments. So he weakened the claim by saying that the meaning of a scientific concept was defined partly by its role in theory and partly by certain tests which verify its application. The giving of these tests *operationally defines* the concept. The tests define its meaning in use, but do not give its whole meaning. For instance, intelligence tests contribute to our understanding of what the concept of intelligence is but they are by no means *all* it is.

This can be contrasted with the operational definition in its strong form which would lead to a statement such as 'intelligence is what intelligence tests measure'. The logical positivists, such as Ayer, would say that we should only study what can be completely nailed down and verified. Everything else is a pseudo-problem, or pseudo-statement. From such views comes the criticism of Freudian theory – that it is untestable therefore it is not a psychological approach that should be studied by psychologists.

Karl Popper made a case against the principle of verification as a criterion for distinguishing between science and non-science. He argued that it was too terribly easy to obtain evidence to support a theory. This is precisely the appeal of Marxist and Freudian theory – they can explain anything. He says he understands what a great feeling of security it gives to think one understands everything:

> Once your eyes were thus opened you saw confirming instances everywhere: the world was full of *verifications* of the theory. Whatever happened always confirmed it. Thus its truth appeared manifest; and unbelievers were clearly people who did not want to see the manifest truth; who refused to see it, either because it was against their class interest, or because of their repressions which were still 'un-analysed' and crying aloud for treatment. (1972:34)

A Marxist is able to find confirmatory evidence every time he opens a newspaper. There are constant indications of the class struggle both in what the paper says and particularly in what it does not say.

As will be discussed further in Chapter 5, Freudian analysts believe that their theory is validated by the 'clinical observations' they make during the course of treatment. Popper was impressed by the power of such observations when he met Alfred Adler. They discussed a case which he had not seen and which did not seem particularly 'Adlerian'. But Adler had no apparent difficulty in analysing it in terms of his theory of inferiority feelings. 'Slightly shocked, I asked him how he could be so sure. "Because of my thousandfold experience", he replied; whereupon I could not help saying: "And with this new case, I suppose, your experience has become thousand-and-one fold."' (Popper, 1972: 35)

In saying that verifiability could not be used as a criterion for distinguishing between science and non-science Popper meant:

> that observations, and even more so observation statements and statements of experimental results, are always *interpretations* of the facts observed; that they are *interpretations in the light of theories*. This is one of the main reasons why it is always deceptively easy to find *verifications* of a theory, and why we have to adopt a highly critical attitude towards our theories if we do not wish to argue in circles: the attitude of trying to *falsify* them. (Popper, 1959: 107)

Popper's concept of falsifiability is important as it is a lively focus of current debate. But he *never* dismissed non-scientific theories as having no value or being meaningless as the logical positivists had misunderstood him to say. For them a non-scientific statement was a meaningless statement. Therefore, if Popper was saying that Marxist and Freudian theories were non-scientific they thought he *must* be saying that they were meaningless garbage deserving to be thrown out of the scientific arena. But, on the contrary, Popper thought non-scientific observations might be of considerable importance. His actual position is best stated in his own words:

> ... 'clinical observations' which analysts naïvely believe confirm their theory cannot do this any more than the daily confirmations which astrologers find in their practice. And as for Freud's epic of the Ego, the Superego, and the

Id, no substantially stronger claim to scientific status can be made for it than for Homer's collected stories from Olympus. These theories describe some facts, but in the manner of myths. They contain most interesting psychological suggestions, but not in a testable form. (Popper, 1972:37)

He saw that such myths may be developed, and become testable and that, historically speaking, nearly all scientific theories originated from myths, and that a myth may contain important anticipations of scientific theories:

I thus felt that if a theory is found to be non-scientific, or 'metaphysical' (as we might say), it is not thereby found to be unimportant, or insignificant, or 'meaningless', or 'nonsensical'. But it cannot claim to be backed by empirical evidence in the scientific sense – although it may easily be, in some genetic sense, the 'result of observation'. (Popper, 1972:38)

Popper went further in arguing that science could never advance if anything that was non-scientific was considered meaningless, since science in the past had emerged from metaphysical or mythical and religious conceptions of the world. As an example of the difference in views between the logical positivists and Popper, take the statement 'mind exists'. For the logical positivists this is an utterly meaningless verbal output. For Popper it is a meaningful statement and might be true but, because there is no known way at present of falsifying the statement, it is not a scientific statement. Magee (1973) has summarized Popper's contribution to our view of scientific method by listing the stages, first, of the traditional view in the following order: 1. observation and method; 2. inductive generalization; 3. hypothesis; 4. attempted verification of hypothesis; 5. proof or disproof; 6. knowledge. Popper replaced this with the stages in the following order: 1. problem (usually a refutation of an existing theory or prediction); 2. proposed solution or new theory; 3. deduction of testable propositions derived from the new theory; 4. tests or attempts to refute by *among other things* observation and experiment; 5. established a preference between competing theories.

So much for the principle of verifiability and the important concept of the operational definition which resulted from Carnap's modification of the principle. For his theory of learning, Hull developed the hypothetico-deductive method, the first principle of which was that 'a satisfactory scientific theory should begin with a set of explicitly stated postulates accompanied by specific or "operational" definitions of the critical terms employed'. (Hull, 1937:5) The second and third principles were:

> 2. From these postulates there should be deduced by the most rigorous logic possible under the circumstances, a series of interlocking theorems covering the major concrete phenomena of the field in question.
> 3. The statements in the theorems should agree in detail with the observationally know facts of the discipline under consideration. If the theorems agree with the observed facts, the system is probably true; if they disagree, the system is false. If it is impossible to tell whether the theorems of a system agree with the facts or not, the system is neither true nor false; scientifically considered, it is meaningless. (Hull, 1937:5)

From these statements comes the psychologist's traditional belief that a scientist first formulates an hypothesis, then makes a prediction on the basis of some experiment designed to test the hypothesis, and looks to the experimental results to show whether the prediction is supported or not.

Hull's attempts to put some flesh and blood on to Watson's skeleton of behaviourism did not have a lasting effect. Skinner came and presented us with the skeleton once more, but a much more clearly defined skeleton. Skinner's model man is

22

'the empty organism'. His man is totally passive and without reason. Our behaviour is determined by its consequences – by the contingencies of reinforcement (see A3). Skinner is by far the most influential figure in psychology today. He is probably as much discussed as Freud was in his day. Whether his influence will continue for as long as has Freud's remains to be seen.

Skinner grew up within an age when behaviourism was at its height – when Hullian theory was but one among many influential attempts to explain the behaviour of man – the object – in mechanistic terms. His experimental analysis of behaviour has a bare minimum of inferential constructs and focuses on man the reactor. He started out with a large number of experiments in which rats and pigeons worked overtime pressing levers or turning heads according to certain *schedules of reinforcement*. A response that is positively reinforced (rewarded) will have an increased probability of occurring again, whereas a response that occurs without being reinforced will be less likely to occur again. An organism's behaviour can be controlled and 'shaped' by the manipulations of environmental reinforcements (see A3, B1).

One of Skinner's arguments against what he calls 'prescientific autonomous man' is that it made man a free agent. He is therefore responsible for his actions and so can be punished by society for wrong-doing. This is not right, Skinner argues, because man's behaviour is determined by the reinforcements his culture has meted out. If society produced the 'right' reinforcements – no punishment would be necessary.

This same concern with responsibility will be found in F7 and F8 and it also comes up again in the discussion of the changing notion about physical and mental well-being in Chapter 3 in this book.

Skinner's psychology can be used to demonstrate a central issue. Some people argue that – theories aside – all accounts of behaviour should be *reflexive*. That is, they should equally

23

well account for the behaviour of the experimenter or theorist as for the person under investigation. Kelly, amongst others, has argued that Skinner is two-faced in this respect. He sees behaviourists as operating a two-tier model – one for the receiver and another for the doer. 'It is not that man is what Skinner makes of him, but rather what Skinner can do man can do – and more. Skinner's subjects are not the model of man; Skinner is.' (Kelly 1969a:136)

Rychlak must be thanked for providing an example of Skinner's duplicity over reflexivity. He cites a *Time* magazine story about Skinner which appeared shortly after the appearance of his book *Beyond Freedom and Dignity*:

> The purpose is clearly to suggest a variation on the 'lonely, mad scientist' theme – the man who wants to control others but who is personally unhappy. I deplore such literary nonsense, but feel there is almost no better way to express how it is possible for a man to have an awareness of his positively reinforcing environment yet evaluate his status in quite other terms. Doubtless Skinner would say there were unnamed contingencies in his contradictory mood, but I feel he is an intensely human person and makes my case (for Skinner being dialectical in behaviour) beautifully in the following, which is a statement attributed to him based on an entry in a personal journal: ... 'Sun streams into our living room. My hi-fi is midway through the first act of *Tristan and Isolde*. A very pleasant environment. A man would be a fool not to enjoy himself in it. In a moment I will work on a manuscript which may help mankind. So my life is not only pleasant, it is earned or deserved. Yet, yet, I am unhappy!' (*Time* 1971:53)

Rychlak continues:

> I rest my case. As one of his fellow-kind I can answer Skinner's challenging query with 'Yes, Professor Skinner, it *is* possible to adopt a norm or its opposite. Man *does*

reason dialectically. You do, as I do. This is how we become intentional animals. This is the source of what freedom from environmental influence we may be said to enjoy'. (Rychlak, 1973:23)

Skinner may be unhappy with himself but many more are unhappy with him. This unhappiness is further expressed in Chapters 4 and 7 of this book. His book *Beyond Freedom and Dignity* has provoked extreme reactions in both the converted and the atheist as it was no doubt *intended* to do. But no! This cannot be the case because, as was shown earlier, there are no intentions (final causes) in nature, and 'proper' scientists only deal with material and/or efficient causes (see p. 11). Perhaps this is another example of the non-reflexive nature of Skinner's scientific view of man. But he does have something to say about intentions in his book:

> The process of operant conditioning presumably evolved when those organisms which were more sensitively affected by the consequences of their behaviour were better able to adjust to the environment and survive. Only fairly immediate consequences could be effective. One reason for this has to do with 'final causes'. Behaviour cannot really be affected by anything which follows it, but if a 'consequence' is immediate, it may overlap the behaviour. A second reason has to do with the functional relation between behaviour and its consequences. The contingencies of survival could not generate a process of conditioning which took into account *how* behaviour produced its consequences. The only useful relation was temporal: a process could evolve in which a reinforcer strengthened any behaviour it followed. But the process was important only if it strengthened behaviour which actually produced results. (Skinner, 1971:120)

Rychlak (1973) points out what a remarkable feat this is on Skinner's part. He seems to be equating the consequences, or what happens after the behaviour, with the final cause or what goes before. Rychlak accuses Skinner of 'cheating' in trying to equate contingency with its final cause or purpose. He quotes Skinner on this point. 'Contingencies *are* ubiquitous; they cover the classical fields of intention and purpose, but in a much more useful way, and they provide alternative formulations of so-called "mental processes".' (Skinner, 1971 : 147)

b) *Man in action*
One path led to a focus on behaviour, the other to man. It was Kant who rebelled against Locke's view of a man who passively assimilates experience. Kant saw man as being active in the world and thus as having some control over his actions.

He was galvanized into action by an argument of one of the British empiricists, David Hume. Hume was objecting to the fact that by now Bacon, Newton, and other scientists had made Aristotle's efficient cause virtually the only cause of interest to science. Hume argued that if the notion of cause was a 'fact', and if knowledge only comes through the senses, how can one account for this 'fact'. One cannot 'see' a cause. He gave the example of billiard ball A which bumps into billiard ball B and the conclusion is drawn that the movement of B is in response to the push of A. But such reasoning, based only on a knowledge of regularities that have happened in the past but which now applied to *all* such events, is *inductive*. Inductive reasoning demands an assumption that transcends the facts. There is a leap from the particular to the general.

Kant took up this idea of the transcendent quality of thought and proceeded to explain sensory experience in terms of mental *categories* (rather than mental activity in terms of sensory experiences as his forerunners had done). We sift sensory experience through these mental categories and by doing so we understand. We are never in a position to perceive reality directly (the noumena) but we see things through our 'mind's eye' (the phenomena). We are an agent rather than an observer and so the only way to explain a piece of behaviour is to find out what the agent has intended to do, or thinks he is doing.

Mind is not the Lockean *tabula rasa* on which whatever we sense is imprinted. On the contrary, what we see is dependent upon our interpretation and classification. One of the questions that such a view raises is what happens when an observer and an agent are confronted by the 'same' event? They may not 'see' the same thing. One of the implications of Kant's thinking is that it is necessary to study human consciousness. And this was indeed a revolutionary thought at the time. For, as everyone then knew, there was no place for consciousness in Newtonian physics and Kant himself agreed that this was the only form of 'true' science.

Kant distinguished between movements and actions. Movements can be studied and explained in terms of causal theories of physics and physiology ('true science'), but the alternatives to studying man from this 'spectator' standpoint is to study him from the point of view of 'agent'. If we do this – study him as a *person* – it will be a very different type of study from that found in physics and physiology. Because its very nature presupposes the existence of the mental 'rules' or conceptions, Kant believed that 'empirical psychology must always remain outside the rank of a natural science properly so called.' (1902:471)

Now we have a model of man who is a person with a particular personal view of the world, and a man who is active. For Kant saw man's will as the ability to act on a mental rule. Our desires and emotions are not blindly and mechanically pushing us to action; rather, action occurs through an act of will, which is 'the faculty of taking a rule of reason for the motive of an action'. (1909:151)

Kant says that the intellect comes by its knowledge in two ways. First, knowledge comes directly from sensory experience – *a posteriori* knowledge, or second, it is innately 'given' – *a priori* knowledge. Reason is different from the intellect as it has no direct relationship with reality. It is reason that provides those 'categories' in the mind through which our understanding of experience can be filtered. Our mind thus brings something to experience and it acts upon experience. Mind is active.

Another aspect of reason, other than understanding, is the 'idea'. Ideas are purely abstract and are beyond and separate from experience. They could *transcend* experience and indulge in flights of fancy, but such flights of fancy cannot result in truth as the conclusions are not subject to demonstration. For Kant still hung on to the notion that Platonic dialectical reasoning was not the preferred method for the discovery of truth, whereas demonstrative reasoning was. He thought that reasoning *should* be tied to the world of reality, but agreed man was quite capable of thinking dialectically. Russell (1959) has pointed out that the dialectic was very important in Kant's philosophy as demonstrated by the fact that the table of categories he proposed is made up of triads 'where the third one listed in each grouping is a combination of the first and second, which are opposites ... The "one and the many" comes back into the history of thought, disguised now as a conceptual scheme for the functioning of mind'. (Rychlak, 1968 : 283)

It was left to Hegel (1770–1831) to fully revive Plato's dialectic. For him there is only one substance – that is mind. But it is not the mind of *man* it is the mind of *men*. It is men who are active rather than passive since all men are part of a community. The mind, as each person knows it, is the mind of a Divine Spirit – it is an objective mind that strives to enter consciousness as history proceeds.

Hegelian phenomenology focuses initially on the particular – the sensory experience of the here and now. This 'particular' is abstract and argument ascends to the absolute, which is the most concrete of all. The method for arriving at knowledge is to argue dialectically in the ways Socrates had described. But Hegel developed a system whereby one could arrive at the correct opposite from which to reason (it had been Aristotle's argument that if one started in error one could end in error). Hegel's method of dialectical reasoning was to start with a 'category', say, *being* (thesis), which objectively requires its opposite, *nothing* (antithesis). From these two poles of meaning a third is deduced – *becoming* (synthesis), resulting in a triad. This triad can then be used to deduce other triads and so the ladder of abstraction is descended deductively and dialectically. In contrast, the inductive reasoner starts at the bottom of the ladder of abstraction and climbs up to higher levels.

Hegel then applied this method of analysis to history. History itself he saw as a form of dialectic. Civilizations fall and rise because each has written in it the seeds of its own destruction in the form of a contradiction. The force of mind that keeps societies and civilizations changing is the Divine Spirit as it comes into self-consciousness. Hegel thus construed activity as spiritual.

Karl Marx (1818–1883) brought this spirit down to earth with a bang. Man is material, Marx argued, but he is spiritual in the sense that he is a self-conscious species–being. There is nothing spiritual about him. Marx can thus be regarded as the first philosopher to bring man firmly and completely down to earth. Man was, for the first time, independent of God.

Marx fully accepted Hegel's dialectic method and described his system of analysing history as *dialectical materialism*. He used Hegel's method of arguing by forming triads made up of the thesis, antithesis, and synthesis. Marx saw the class struggle as consisting of the *bourgeois* (thesis) and the *proletariat* (antithesis), with the tension of opposites being resolved by a revolution leading to the establishment of a classless society which was called *communism* (synthesis). The dialectic now became more than a method for arriving at truth, it became a tool to be used in the class war that *must* end in the victory of communism over capitalism for that is

29

the nature of things. Just as Hegel saw the Divine Spirit as a force producing change, because of its compulsion to 'know itself', so for Marx there is a similar compulsion about the evolution of material things. Communism would happen because the dialectic is a universal logic.

The influence of Marx's philosophy is evident in radical psychology. You will find discussion of such things as the oppression of women, homosexuals and 'patients' mentioned in subsequent chapters of this book but particularly in F8.

One disenchantment that followers of Marxist philosophy have experienced is in the value of Freudian theory as a means of studying the individual. Marx explained 'social man' but had nothing to say about 'personal man'. The Marxist is thus looking for a theory that will enable him to see 'personal man' in relation to his social environment. But Freud tried to understand man in terms of unconscious processes, which made him irrational and passive, and did little indeed to describe man in relation to what goes on around him. Brooks argues that the sort of psychology Marxists are looking for is 'one that can be defined on one level as the study of the mode of relatedness of this individual social being to his or her situation: ... It includes in its definition the concept that one cannot understand individuals without understanding the world they live in and the meaning it has for them.' (1973: 370) In this definition we can see Kant's influence – trying not to understand the realities of the world (the noumena), but the individual's understanding of them (the phenomena).

Perhaps this is why some Marxists have turned their attention to the philosophical and psychological system of George Kelly (see D3, F3, F7, F8). Kelly's model man is very similar to Kant's model man. Both see us as looking out at life through 'goggles'. Our view of the world is influenced by the already existing system for organizing the sensory experience. Our experience is either sifted through 'mental categories' (Kant) or personal constructs (Kelly). In both cases there is no hope for us to see the 'real' world, we see only our interpretations of it. The essential notion in the theory (expressed in a Fundamental Postulate and elaborated by eleven corollaries) is that 'Man looks at his world through transparent patterns or templates which he creates and then attempts to fit over the realities of which the world is composed. The fit is not always very good. Yet without such patterns the world appears to be such an undifferentiated homogeneity that man is unable to make any sense out of it.' (Kelly, 1955:9)

Kelly's theory is also clearly a dialectical one:

Personal construct theory assumes, among other things, that any construct used by man is, psychologically speaking, a bi-polar affair. One does not understand a personal construct simply by apprehending some basis of *similarity* between objects; he must understand the basis of *distinction* as well. Both similarity and contrast are involved. So we look for the grounds upon which certain matters can be judged as similar to each other, and, by the same token, stand in meaningful contrast to certain other objects within the construct's range of convenience. Stated in Hegelian terms this is to say no thesis is complete without its antithesis. Perhaps I should add that I am aware that this dialectical form goes back a good deal further than Hegel, perhaps as far as the pre-Socratic philosopher Anaximander. Be that as it may, I am not so much concerned with the classical logic of the dialectic as I am with its psychological appropriateness in describing how man characteristically functions. (1969b:169)

Kelly's model man is a man of action. There is no need for a concept of motivation because, by his very nature, he is a form of motion. He is also an agent and not a reactor. He goes about the business of understanding his world doing the same things scientists do. He interprets events in his environment. That is, he comes to a situation with hypotheses about the world. He tests these hypotheses by behaving in a certain way and then looks to see whether or not predictions derived from these hypotheses have been validated. The evidence he gets from one such experiment will influence how he approaches the next and therefore whether he changes his behaviour. Kelly's approach to change has been discussed in Chapter 7 under the heading 'phenomenologists', although he never accepted that this described his views.

It was Hegel who first used the term *phenomenology* to describe a philosophical system but it is Husserl (1859–1938) who is usually referred to as 'the father of phenomenology'. He argued that, since we can only know the *phenomenal* and never the *noumenal* world (see p. 26), science has to be based on *intersubjectivity*. We can only gain understanding of the thoughts and feelings of another when we share the *meaning* that experience has for him. Husserl thought that to describe the human condition properly we need a new method of scientific investigation. His method was to try and capture the 'essence' of meaning – what words 'really' mean. To achieve this, he used Kant's idea that man has the capacity to *transcend* his sensory experience. He has the capacity to turn back on himself as if he were an object. Husserl used this procedure to investigate the individual's phenomenal world and called it *transcendental phenomenology*. But apart from a method, Husserl did not produce any substantial body of knowledge.

It was the Gestalt psychologists who were the first to use the notions of phenomenology extensively. Their major concern was with sensation and perception and with finding out how man organizes his perceptual world. Over the years they described a series of laws that explained how the phenomenal field is organized (see A4).

This path has led us to reject inductive reasoning, demonstrative reasoning, and the methods of Newtonian physics for a psychology of man. In its place we have suggestions that psychology should be the study of the actor as a *person* rather than as object with his 'bits' of behaviour.

III *A summary of some constructs and metaconstructs*

When attempting to see similarities and differences between theories or concepts or ideas, we often use metaconstructs. The prefix 'meta' comes from the Greek and has come to mean that something is of a higher order, it overrides what has gone before, it transcends all below it. Thus we can look at what has been discussed with some constructs that give such an overview.

a) *Models or images of man*

Models are simply ways of ordering ideas, of organizing events into patterns. For instance, a theoretician may use concepts and talk of man *as if* he were talking about a computer. This is not to say that the theoretician actually thinks man *is* a computer, but just that he finds it useful to use terms such as input and output, circuits and so forth (see A1). Thus, with any theory of man it is useful to analyse the concepts that are being used and then work out how the theoretician is 'seeing' man.

Models become particularly important when the theory is applied. In this unit, much of the emphasis of the applied work is in the clinical field, which means that the theories are being applied to bring about change in those in psychological distress. The theoretical model is important because it will determine exactly how the clinician will go about his job of helping an individual change. Three general models are used to demonstrate this point – the Freudian or dynamic model, the behaviourist or 'technician' model, and the phenomenological or the 'action-man' model.

b) *Motivation*

This is a concept popular in psychology and it can be seen as a descendant of Aristotle's *efficient cause*. Since much psychological thinking is still tied to the natural sciences, some 'energy' had to be brought in from somewhere to account for the fact that people 'do' things. In physics it is a force, so why not in psychological science? In his attempt to describe people, Freud had psychic energy as one of his fundamental theoretical concepts. Thus when a concept of motivation is used the view is of a man who is driven.

But an alternative point of view is that this construct is unnecessary. Kelly (1962) has pointed out that we do not have to *conceptualize* man in this way. Maybe we could think of him as a form of motion himself. If we do so, then there is no need for the concept of motivation at all. Man acts or behaves because he is alive. He is not driven, he drives himself. What we have to explain is why each person drives himself as he does.

One of the many ways in which this unit differs from the previous unit (E) on applied psychology is in the use of this concept of motivation. Man in industry is often described as being motivated. He is pushed and pulled by rewards and punishments within the industrial system.

The whole history of psychology can be seen in terms of a metaconstruct concerning the passivity of man as he is conceptualized by the theorists. Is he best construed as a passive responder (as in behaviourism) or as an actor, a person who actively construes and interprets events in his world and acts in terms of these personal interpretations?

c) *Deductive versus inductive reasoning*
Inductive reasoning describes the situation in which we reason from the particular case to the general case. In terms of levels of abstraction, we go from a lower level to a higher level. The jump up the ladder always involves a logical leap or, to give it its proper name, an *inference*.

Deductive reasoning is the opposite. It occurs when we reason from a general case to a particular case. We may have a theory which is at a higher level of abstraction and deduce a proposition that is at a lower level. Popper expresses himself strongly on this point:

> The belief that science proceeds from observation to theory is still so widely and so firmly held that my denial of it is often met with incredulity ... But in fact the belief that we can start with pure observations alone, without anything in the nature of a theory is absurd. (1972:46)

As an example he tells how he tried to convince a group of physics students of this. He told them to take pencil and paper – observe – and write down what they had observed. The students immediately asked *what* they were to observe. The instruction was obviously absurd. 'Observation is always selective. It needs a chosen object, a definite task, an interest, a point of view, a problem.' (1972:46) We could consider the activity of being a scientist as a typical example of the sort of activity which any psychological theory has to explain. Thus our particular view of how science is carried out is an instance of our general view of the nature of man. The notion that science is conducted inductively implies a passive recipient of evidence; that it is conducted deductively, an active construer of reality.

2
Give us the tools and we will finish the job

I The job

What do psychologists think they are in the business for? As you may have gathered from the preceding chapter, they are not too sure. But I think it fair to say that those in 'mainstream' psychology believe they are in the fact-finding business. But so perhaps is the 'man-in-the-street'. The former seeks facts that he thinks will ultimately lead to general laws of human behaviour, while the latter seeks facts that will enable him to reshuffle his rules (mental categories, concepts, constructs) so that he will be able to predict future events more accurately than in the past.

The models of man used in modern psychology can be traced back many centuries, and this is equally true of experimentation. From Aristotle came the 'mainstream' psychology of today, with its experimental format concentrating on the recording of observations and the classification of objects and events. The precise modern experimental approach, though, came from Galileo, Bacon, and Newton. But Newton only focused on part of what Galileo was saying. For while Galileo did indeed believe that nature was a perfect machine – and because of that one could predict and control its motions –

Galileo also believed in the power of the intellect (albeit a mathematical intellect) and man's ability to apply it in his research. For Galileo, an experiment was only needed when one reached a parting of the ways in one's thinking.

Bolton (1975) points to the re-emergence of Galileo's original definition of the experiment – that *it is a question put to nature*:

> as in Relativity Theory, for example, where an experiment involves activity and a theory for interpreting that activity. In brief, an experiment is an action. Kelly's dictum that behaviour is an experiment is only an extension of this idea, an extension one would expect a psychologist to make, for our experimental activities do not cease when we leave the laboratory. Rather what we call scientific experiments are a relatively small and special case of relating to and finding out about the world in which we live.

Today you will find experiments carried out in two ways (see A8). One in which there are no hypotheses, such as when a group of people are given a number (battery) of tests to 'see what happens'. The other is when the experimenter has some specific hypothesis he wants to test and which he has derived from some particular viewpoint and he seeks to verify (or falsify) his hypothesis by an experiment.

But one of the sad things about the facts so gathered is that they very rarely mix well together. This is sad because some people really do sincerely believe that by piling fact upon fact we will progress step by step to the final 'truth'.

The facts that psychologists produce do not add up meaningfully because *either* there is no theory on which the piece of research has been based *or* psychologist A's theory is different from psychologist B's theory and the concepts used by each are not cross-referable (see F7).

An alternative to the brick by brick approach (which Kelly calls *accumulative fragmentalism*), based on the assumption that meaning is derived from below, is the Kantian model that sees meaning coming from above (which Kelly calls *constructive alternativism*). As Kelly explains in his paper 'Strategies of Psychological Research', the step after the experiment shows up differences in approach.

> To the accumulative fragmentalist the next step is to find another nugget of truth ... To the constructive alternativist the next step is to see if he can improve his hypothesis, perhaps by formulating his questions in new ways or by pursuing the implications of some fresh assumption that occurred to him when he was writing up the conclusions to his last experiment. (1965:10)

Our 'man-in-the-street' (and perhaps our Kantian psychologist) makes a prediction about how Joe Bloggs is going to behave and looks with interest to see if his prediction is accurate. If it is, then he might ask himself if he could perhaps have had an hypothesis that would have led to an even *more* accurate prediction of Joe Bloggs's behaviour. He is thus a man constantly trying out new and, he hopes, better ways of predicting events in his world. He is a creative man. Our 'mainstream' psychologist has little such imagination – he goes from one fact to the next. One of the central themes in John Shotter's book (F7) is the art of science and the difference it makes to conceptualize man as playing an active part in his world as opposed to being passively played upon by events.

Associated with these two different approaches to experimentation is the argument about measuring some aspect of one person – and so coming to know more about an individual – or objectively obtaining general facts from large numbers of people telling us little about the individual. For the former approach there is the spine-chilling word *idiography* and for the latter *nomothesis*. Idio comes from the Greek meaning *own*, personal, private, and so idiography becomes the study of a person's own or personal, private 'signature'. Nomothetic originally meant *law-giving* and has been used to describe procedures or methods that are designed to discover general laws.

But whichever method one decides to adopt, when one carries out an experiment or does research, it is necessary to collect *data*. To help him in his task, the psychologist has what he considers to be a well stocked tool-bag.

II The tools

There are many ways of killing a cat. Or so the saying goes. First know your cat; study the various ways in which it can be killed; select the best tool for the purpose in hand. But there are certain things that are common to virtually all standard psychological research, be it to study cats or men.

a) *A few general issues about experiments*
When the subject is the object. One approach to the problem would be to carry out carefully designed experiments with cats in our laboratory so as to find the most effective way of producing the desired end. We study the cat as an object (although it will be called a subject) so as to bring its behaviour under our *control*.

The minute we call a human being an object we have dehumanized him. But by this verbal sleight of hand psychologists have managed to keep this fact from themselves until relatively recent times.

Those pesky variables. When trying to get some knowledge about our cats, the behaviour that we try and predict will be the *dependent variable*, and the method we employ to produce that predicted behaviour will be the *independent variable* (see A8).

By placing our object of study in the laboratory we have also got to *control* all variables except the one in which we are interested. It is important that our objects do not vary

39

haphazardly in relation to such human things as age, social class, intelligence. But there seems to be a little problem here too. Surely it is the human objects who vary *in relation to* age, social class and intelligence? These are static categories or continua into or along which human beings can vary. It is not the human beings who stand motionless in line, while age, social class, or intelligence vary in relation to them. Our terminology seems to have got upside down again.

Two and two make? One of the most fascinating tools that psychologists possess is 'statistics' (see A9). Statistics has the fascination for psychologists that the piping has for the cobra in its basket as it sways to and fro. Do not get me wrong. I am not arguing that there should be no statistics in psychology. I am arguing that we should keep a close watch on our use of them and see that they remain a tool which we use for specific purposes; we should not let them become our master in dictating the sort of research we should do. As an example of what I mean by this is the comment made by an eminent research worker not so long ago: 'it is a brave man who sets out to test an hypothesis as you cannot be sure of getting an answer. I prefer to use the empirical approach and factor analysis because this guarantees results.'

He was wrong to say that you cannot guarantee getting an answer when you test an hypothesis. What he meant was that you may not get a result that is *statistically significant*. For most psychologists would, in their merrier moments, agree that there is a fatal fascination with the magical '5% level'. If your experiment enables you to conclude that the result you have obtained could have occurred by chance only one time in twenty, then you have a nugget of truth that can be reported in the literature. If it could have occurred by chance one time in nineteen then you have failed and few journals will accept your report. This is the psychologist's version of Mr Micawber's recipe for happiness: 'Annual income twenty pounds, annual expenditure nineteen nineteen six, result happiness. Annual income twenty pounds, annual expenditure twenty pounds ought and six, result misery.'

Apart from this rather frivolous comment on tests of significance, there are many far more serious ones.

The testing of the null hypothesis has been attacked by many psychologists. The basic idea is that we start off by saying 'there is *no difference* between these two groups of Subjects'. When we find our test of significance gives us the probability that the *actual difference* is likely to occur by chance less than one time in twenty, then we are in a position to reject the null hypothesis (that there is no difference) – for we have clearly shown there is. One difficulty appears to be that the larger the sample we use, the greater is the likelihood of our finding a difference: '... if the null hypothesis is not rejected, it is usually because the N is too small. If enough data are gathered, the hypothesis will generally be rejected. If rejection of the null hypothesis were the real intention in psychological experiments, there usually would be no need to gather data.' (Nunnally, 1960:643)

But Bolles points out that even if we obtain the treasured 5% significance level 'statistical rejection of the null hypothesis tells the scientist only what he was already quite sure of – the animals (subjects) are not behaving randomly. The fact that the null hypothesis can be rejected ... does not give E (the experimenter) an assurance ... that his particular hypothesis is true, but only that some alternative to the null hypothesis is true.' (1962:642)

The Experimenter effect. We have got our Subject and Experimenter in the laboratory with variables controlled and statistics at the ready. But all is still not straightforward.

One issue in psychological research concerns the extent to which (if at all) the Experimenter comes into the picture and affects experimental results. If psychology is about people it should be able to account as well for the behaviour of the Experimenter as for the Subject. It used to be thought that all the Experimenter had to do was to control those 'pesky' variables (all those things that make the individual unique) so that any differences between group A and group B would be attributable to the 'treatment' given to one group and not to the other. Orne (1962) was one of the first to show that the experimental situation is a social one and that Subjects have expectations. First of all he asked some acquaintances to do five 'press-ups'. They all regarded him as slightly mad and asked *why* they should do so. He next asked another group of people to take part in an experiment which would involve their doing five 'press-ups'. They simply asked him where and when.

Since then Rosenthal and other workers have done a great deal of work looking at the effect of both the Subject's and the Experimenter's expectations on the results obtained in laboratory experiments. In one such experiment Rosenthal (1967) gave a group of Experimenters the same instructions on how to carry out a study in which the Subjects were to judge the expressions on faces in ten photographs. But, half the Experimenters were told that previous research had shown the 'well-established fact' that faces tended to be rated as belonging to 'successful' people, while the others were told that people generally considered the photographs to be of 'unsuccessful' people. Both groups of Experimenters had Subjects that gave them – the Experimenters – what they had been led to expect, although all the Subjects had been given the same instructions.

Hampden-Turner has criticized the typical method of experimentation because of the one-sided attempt at control:

You can only get answers to those questions you are asking. Questions about relationships of trust, equality and dialogue between the investigator and his subject are not being asked, since they offend against current conceptions of good methodology. But power over people in a laboratory can *only* lead (if it leads anywhere) to a technology of behaviour control. The results which flow from the unilateral inputs of the experimenter are only applicable to those exercising unilateral inputs in our culture. (1971:5)

From such statements and from the work of Rosenthal and others like him, psychologists are being brought face to face with political and ethical issues.

Research and deception. Rosenthal's 'Experimenters' were deceived by him but the issue of deception has gathered momentum since the experiments of Stanley Milgram (1974). These experiments on obedience, carried out over a period of years, gave evidence of psychological harm being done to Subjects. Deceit is one thing, harm another. Milgram's Subjects were required to make a person learn by administering shocks whenever a mistake was made. 'The 'learner' was part of the deception and, every time a shock was administered, he gave an appropriate response to pain although he actually received no shock at all. The Subject had a number of shock levels to choose from, ranging from mild to very severe, and was ordered to continue with the experiment even when the 'learner' was begging for mercy.

Many of the Subjects became very anxious and agitated as the experiment progressed and some were particularly disturbed at the realization that they were prepared to inflict suffering on another human being in the interest of science. The argument is that if we were to study people instead of objects, the risk of doing harm to people would be greatly reduced.

Such work as Milgram's led to a code of ethics being drawn up which, in turn, led to a very unusual *independent variable*. It was observed that the ethics suggested in the 'Ethical Standards for Research with Human Subjects' (Cook *et al*, 1972) had not themselves been made subject to scientific inquiry: 'a modest irony – although there is much feeling that changing the ethical codes under which experimental data are collected could eventually change the very nature of psychological knowledge itself.' (Resnick and Schwarz, 1973: 134) Four of the principles involve telling the Subject the purpose of the experiment. For example, principle 1.421 states: 'The subject must be informed in advance of all aspects of the research that bear directly on his own experience in it, including (a) any treatment that he is to receive, (b) any data that will be collected from him, and (c) the magnitude of the investment that is being asked of him such as the time involved, etc.'

Resnick's experiment, in which ethical standards were to be the independent variable, was one on verbal conditioning. The 'ethical' group were told the purpose of the experiment for which they were being asked to volunteer. This meant they had to be given the facts about verbal conditioning experiments:

You will be asked to come into a room where you will be given 100 3×5 inch cards, one at a time on each of which is printed six pronouns: I, We, You, They, She, He, and a verb. These pronouns will appear in random order from one card to the next and the instructions that will be given you at the time will be to compose a sentence using the verb that is printed on that particular card, and to begin the sentence with one of the six pronouns. If you begin your sentence with either the pronoun 'I' or 'We', the experimenter will say 'good' or 'mmm-hmmm', or 'okay'. Previous findings using this method have shown that subjects will increase their use of the reinforced pronouns over the 100 trials to a significant degree beyond the level that they were using these pronouns in the initial trials ... (Resnick and Schwartz, 1973: 135)

The 'non-ethical' group (those not told the purpose of the experiment) showed typical increase in the use of the reinforced pronouns while the 'ethical' Subjects showed significant *negative* conditioning (they decreased rather than increased the number of times they used the pronouns that were reinforced!). The authors suggest several reasons for this state of affairs, including boredom or suspicion. They conclude: 'We should be highly cautious in imposing additional methodological limits on our already overtaxed scientific methods. Are we ready to accept a qualitatively different ordering of reality which may result from changing our methods of investigating it?' Some say 'yes'.

The argument centres on the increasing concern for the individual to be a subject – a human subject – rather than a dehumanized object. A human must be allowed to sum up a situation and act according to his interpretation of that situation.

Another point that should interest us all is the extraordinary paucity of information (facts) that psychologists have gathered about how human beings go about their business of living. Could it be that the process of laboratory experimentation has itself militated against the finding of valuable human information? The point at issue is succinctly summarized by Beloff: 'Indeed it is debatable whether, during its century of existence as an independent science, psychology has yet produced one single fact of any fundamental importance about human behaviour or the human mind.' (1973:20)

It may be that the thousands of man-hours spent in carrying out laboratory experiments do no real harm to anyone and that psychologists are playing some enormous confidence trick on society – and this has indeed been said. But this is not totally true. I am sure that you will find within the covers of many of the books of *Essential Psychology* information that helps you in understanding others. But when you come across such information, perhaps you will pause a moment to see whether it came from one of the typical experimental laboratory settings or from the ideas of one of the several imaginative psychologists following Kant's view of man, such as Jean Piaget (see C2) or George Kelly (see D3), and then consider the implications this information has for the way *you* interpret the findings.

b) *Field observations*

As a method of collecting data outside the laboratory this is fairly straightforward procedure (see C1). The observer observes children at play, babies' early movements, animals in their natural environment. No account is taken of what the child, animal, adult, thinks he is doing. His various behaviours are observed and totted up in some carefully designed way. But the natural environment can also become the laboratory. A good example of this is Piaget's work. His observations of a few young children led him to formulate certain ideas about the intellectual development of children which were then tested. For instance, he hypothesized that the young child has no concept about the permanence of objects. So he would take the ball the child was playing with and, in front of the child's gaze, place the ball under a chair so that it was no longer visible to the child. The test of his hypothesis would be whether the child searched for the ball or not. Piaget was therefore doing more than just observing and totting up behaviours. He was attempting to understand how that child might be seeing its world.

So also in environmental psychology, where field experiments have produced valuable results. Details of such procedures are to be found in F5.

c) *Survey methods*

This is one of the most widely used methods in the social sciences and is particularly relevant to Frost's account of how attitudes to products are obtained from consumers (F6) and Lee's account of the relationship between people and their environments (F5). In a sense, it is like the method of field observation in that the attitudes or behaviours of large numbers of people are noted in the 'field'. But the method of observation is specific and sophisticated. The person who stops you while you are rushing to catch a train and asks whether you have ever heard of B. F. Skinner or H. J. Eysenck may well be conducting a survey into how far the thoughts of (in)famous psychologists have affected the lives of 'the man in the street'.

It is important to distinguish between the methods of experiment and of survey. In the latter there is no hypothesis, no aim to test anything, no prediction. The aim is to obtain information concerning an aspect of life. Care must be taken to ensure that the answers obtained do indeed answer the basic question under investigation. How the questions are phrased is vitally important. In his article 'Asking Silly Questions', Roiser nicely points out the problem.

> Some time ago I was asked, as a subject, to fill in a questionnaire drawn up by a well-known social psychologist. It was entitled 'The Student and Society'. I recall a feeling of intense annoyance on finding the following item: 'I am in favour of destroying the present political system even without knowing what will replace it'. My pencil hovered nihilistically over the response 'strongly agree', then wavered uneasily between 'mildly agree' and 'cannot answer'. In vain did I search the questionnaire for a reasonable expression of my views. Caricatures of extremity and moderation predominated, intermingled with potted homilies and laughable simplifications. I added a side of my own views on the back, but I doubt whether they were quantifiable, as that term is generally understood by psychologists. (1974: 101)

While the form of the questions asked is of paramount importance in conducting surveys, so is *sampling*. It is obviously not possible to question every person in the population under consideration. A representative sample has to be selected so that conclusions based on the data collected from the sample are valid for the whole population. Clearly many variables will have to be considered; age, social class, parents' nationality, intelligence, marital status and much else besides. How you draw your sample and the kinds of conclusions that can be drawn from the data are the province of *sampling theory*.

d) *Test method*

The concept of sampling also crops up when we consider psychological tests. There are tests everywhere and in all contexts. Rosemary Shakespeare (see F2) discusses several types of test, but one that is important in handicap (and elsewhere) is the intelligence test (see D4).

This is an example of a nomothetic test *par excellence*. Right from the start when the Frenchman Binet devised the first intelligence test, the aim has been to compare a person's score with the range of scores obtained by a representative sample of people of the individual's own age. There is, of course, no such 'thing' as intelligence. It is simply a concept that some people have found useful in describing certain types of behaviour. Rosemary Shakespeare is concerned with intelligence tests given to children and adults to determine just how handicapped *in relation to others* a particular child or adult is.

Intelligence tests can be used as an example of some of the concepts involved in psychometric testing generally. They must be *valid* and *reliable*. To be valid the test must measure what most of us would recognize as 'intelligence'. It would be no good giving a test to a group of people in the fond belief that it was measuring their intellectual ability and finding out that it was actually measuring their ability to see the funny side of life. Validity can be assessed in a number of ways, but all result in a *validity correlation coefficient*. The statistical procedure for deriving correlations is described in detail in A9. Basically, a correlation is a measure of the degree of relationship between any two scores or measures. Thus, to determine whether a test is valid or not, you might give it to children aged thirteen and predict that their test scores would relate to the marks they obtained three years later in a particular examination. Those with high marks would have had a high score on the intelligence test and those with low marks a low intelligence test score.

Reliability is also measured by the method of correlation, and again there are several ways of finding out how reliable or consistent a test is. If a test is given to the same person on two occasions the degree of relationship between these two sets of scores is the *reliability correlation coefficient*. While it is obviously important that an intelligence test should be consistent over time, there is the question of how long a time? For clearly, if a test showed itself to be reliable over twenty years, it is in effect saying that it is measuring something that is totally resistant to change. That is all to the good if your model man is seen as being unchangeable by his environment. But if once we accept that people are going about the business of living and are capable of constant change – what price reliability then?

Apart from being shown to be reliable and valid, tests have scores that are normally distributed (see Fig. 2.1 (a) below). This bell-shaped distribution of scores is called *normal* because of its symmetrical shape. Compare this with the curve in Fig. 2.1 (b) which has a tail jutting out on one side only. The penalty for this tail is to be called *skewed*.

Intelligence, as measured in tests, is normally distributed. This means that there will be as many people with a very high intelligence score as there will be with a very low score. Sometimes for practical purposes, those with scores below 70 are called mentally *handicapped*.

But there is one further piece of information that is required before IQ scores can be discussed intelligently. That is the *standard deviation* (see A9). Normal distributions can have various shapes and it is possible to describe a particular shape by knowing the *mean* and the *standard deviation* of the distribution [see Fig 2.1 (a)]. For *any* normal distribution, roughly 68% of all sources will fall between +1.0 and −1.0 standard deviations of the mean; 95% of all scores between

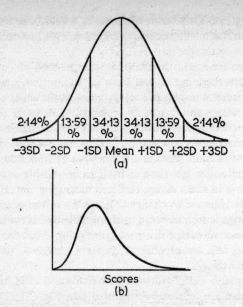

Fig. 2.1 *Two distributions of scores: a) normal b) skewed*

+2.0 and −2.0 standard deviations; and 99.7% between
+3.0 and −3.0. Supposing the mean of the test were 100
and the standard deviation 15, then 68% of the people would
get between 115 and 85, 95% between 130 and 70, and
99.7% between 145 and 55. To see what a difference this
standard deviation can make, look at Table 1.1.

The object lesson is that a person with a score of 145 on a
test with a standard deviation of 15 is in exactly the same
position *relative* to the normal population as is the person with
a score of 175 on a test with a standard deviation of 25.

Having categorized the person as mentally handicapped on
the basis of an intelligence test result, there seems to be an
end of its usefulness in that context. For it tells nothing about
the individual's adjustments to the people in his world, his
likes and dislikes and so forth. Also, like diagnosis in the

	68%	95%	99·7%
standard deviation	+1·0	+2·0	+3·0
15	85–115	70–130	55–145
20	80–120	60–140	40–160
25	75–125	50–150	25–175

Table 1.1 *Range of scores for three different standard deviations on three tests with a mean of 100*

world of mental illness, the pinning of an I.Q. label on a child can produce stagnation. Some years ago it was certainly the case that a label of subnormality was sufficient to have the child placed in a hospital where the most he could hope for was to be looked after physically and kept occupied. It is only relatively recently that people have begun to stop thinking of the I.Q. as something fixed. Twenty years ago Kelly stated the position like this:

> The child who is nailed down to the I.Q. continuum has just that much less chance of changing his teacher's opinion about him. If he is 'low', his unorthodox constructive ventures will never be given a thoughtful hearing; if he is 'high' his stupidities will be indulged as the eccentricities of genius. In formulating the construct of the I.Q. we may have become enmeshed in the same net that immobilizes many a patient; we may have been caught in the web of our own construct system. Having been so careful to pin all persons down to a continuum with respect to which they can never change, we may now be confronted with a product of our own handiwork – a world full of people whom we cannot conceive of as changing, whom we can do nothing about! Is not I.Q. a distressingly unfertile construct after all? Should we not, therefore, take better care when we create the design specifications for future diagnostic constructs? (1955 : 454)

Just how effective 'changing his teacher's opinions' can be was demonstrated some years later by Rosenthal and Jacobson (1968) when they led teachers to believe that there were some 'potential bloomers' in the class. These were children who, the teachers were told, were not doing too well at the moment, but were basically bright. And, lo and behold! the children's I.Q.'s increased several points.

The intelligence score should be just a starting point. It is not the end of the road.

Several intelligence tests are based upon factor analysis. This is a statistical procedure that is referred to in F5 and is a concept of major importance in F6. You may also sometimes see the phrase *multivariate analysis* used. This is the more global concept that includes factor analysis.

Let us suppose we want to understand what makes 'teachers tick'. We may decide that each is unique. If so, then our job has finished before it starts. But we may have reached a decision that there are qualities in common that make one group of teachers different from the rest. If so, the job is to describe these qualities and then to see how they are used to differentiate between the teachers.

You might decide that one axis for differentiating among the teachers is *sex*. So you group the teachers at the appropriate *male* or *female* end of the continuum. Next you may have noted that some are *serious* and others *light-hearted*, so you unscramble them from the sex dimension and group them at one end or other of the *serious–light-hearted* axis. You can go on unscrambling and re-grouping your teachers along as many axes as you think are appropriate. They may be differentiated as *good* versus *bad*; *authoritarian* versus *easygoing*; *sexy* versus *not sexy*; *old* versus *young*. Having done all this you have got a fairly complex description of each teacher. Each can be thought of as sitting in a particular point in this multidimensional psychological space you have constructed.

Exactly the same sort of thing can be done with intelligence test items, or answers to a questionnaire concerning a market research product or people's attitudes to large buildings. It is a statistical procedure for organizing complex data in a relatively simple manner – providing there is a tame computer near at hand.

The problem or danger is that you may regard these dimensions as the only ones there could be. You could cement them into a test that can be applied to all new teachers. In this case new teachers can only vary along the dimensions obtained from an analysis of the old teachers.

Apart from this possible 'hardening of the categories' another argument levelled against such nomothetically-derived tests is that these factors or test norms may not describe any one individual. They may be all right when used on groups of people but may give an erroneous picture when applied to an individual. A clear example of this problem comes from experimental psychology. Baloff and Becker (1967) showed that the learning curve based on the average learning scores of a number of individuals does not resemble learning curves of any individual. Fig. 2.2 shows the average curve and one of the individual curves that contributed to the average.

An example of the idiographic method and one which is discussed in several books in *Essential Psychology* is repertory grid technique. This was originally described by Kelly (1955) to provide a means whereby the relationships between units of his theory – the constructs – could be described in mathematical terms.

The description of the way in which one might go about analysing differences between teachers is also a description of how Kelly sees constructs interrelating. Constructs are dimensions that we place over events in order to make sense of those events. They are ways in which we organize happenings in our personal environments. We, each one of us, look at life through a set of goggles made up of the constructs in our construct system. If the dimension *tolerant–intolerant* is important to you, you will place it over the new person you meet and decide whether he is best described as tolerant or intolerant.

To find out the construct dimensions you used to differen-

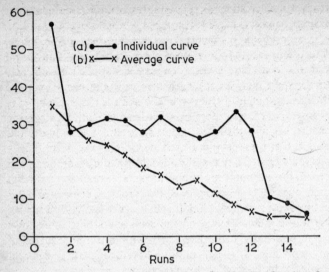

Fig. 2.2 *Redrawn from Baloff and Becker (1967) showing the average learning curve and one of the individual curves contributing to the average*

tiate among your teachers and then to calculate the mathematical relationships between the dimensions, you might proceed like this. First you make a list of teachers – perhaps eight of them. Now take three, and ask yourself in what important way two of them are alike and thereby different from the third. You might say that two are men and one is a woman. That is your first construct dimension – *man* with its opposite *woman*. You can write this construct into your grid along the top as in Fig. 2.3. You now take three different teachers and ask yourself the same question. Your answer might be two are *serious* and the other *light-hearted* – and this next construct is written into the grid. So with another three teachers you might now differentiate between them as *good* versus *bad* teachers. Obviously you cannot go on taking a completely different triad each time if you have only eight

54

| | ELEMENTS | | | | | | | |
| CONSTRUCTS | | | | teachers | | | | |
	A	B	C	D	E	F	G	H
masculine	2	1	5	4	3	6	8	7
serious	6	2	1	3	8	4	5	7
good teacher								
authoritarian								
sexy								
old								
gets on with others								
lonely								
like me in character								
like I hope to become								

Fig. 2.3 *A matrix of rankings for a repertory grid with teachers as elements*

teachers. But you can ensure that each contains one different *element* (teacher) on each elicitation.

You may decide to stop when you have elicited seven or eight constructs from the teacher elements. But you could go on to 'ladder' two or three of them. This process of laddering is in effect asking yourself (or someone else) to abstract from one conceptual level to another. You could ladder from *man–woman*, but it might be easier to start off with *serious–light-hearted*. Ask yourself which you would prefer to be – *serious* or *light-hearted*. You might reply *light-hearted*. Now pose the question 'why'. Why would you rather be a *light-hearted* person than a *serious* person? Perhaps the answer would be that *light-hearted* people *get on better with others* than do *serious* people. Ask yourself 'why' again. Why do you want to be the sort of person who gets on better with others? Perhaps it transpires that you think that people who do not get on well with others are *lonely*. In this way you elicit more constructs but ones that stand on the shoulders of those previously elicited. Whatever constructs you have obtained can be put into the grid in Fig. 2.3.

If you have decided to do a rank order form of grid, you take the first construct *man–woman* and rank the teachers in terms of the construct. Now you may have difficulty! You could rank in terms of masculinity or femininity but you must realize that you have reworded the construct. There should be less of a problem ranking the teachers from more to less serious and more to less good at teaching.

In the rank order form of grid, you really only deal with one pole of the construct, that is, rank from most to least masculine, most to least serious. As you can see from Fig. 2.3, it is also possible to supply constructs that you think may be of special interest. In this case, two aspects of the self have been supplied.

An alternative to ranking the people would have been to rate each person on a 7-point or 5-point scale in relation to each construct. The merits and demerits of these and other forms of grid are discussed in Bannister and Mair (1968).

The principles of analysis for ranking or rating are substantially the same. Each set of ratings or rankings would be correlated with every other, so that a matrix of correlations would be obtained. Various statistical procedures can then be applied – including factor analysis. Another popular method is to analyse the matrix into its principle components. Such a method has been extensively used and developed by Slater (1972).

Although originally designed as a method for studying the individual (i.e. as an idiographic method) it can also be used nomothetically. If both constructs and elements are supplied by the investigator, then the rankings or ratings of individuals can be averaged for a group of people just as they can for any other set of scores. It is mainly used in this nomothetic way in market research and environmental studies but is not so common in the clinical setting where the information about individuals is more often required.

What all this talk of tests boils down to is that it is horses for courses. The job of the researcher is to work out the purpose of his research according to his particular conceptual model and then choose the tool best suited to his purpose. If he wants to assess ability then he applies his expertise to choosing the test best suited to assessing that particular ability. If he wants to understand a particular individual's view of the world he will choose between the several tools available for that purpose. Conversely, if he is wedded to a particular tool he will find purposes for its use and may or may not 'buy' the model that originally went with that particular tool.

3
Health and illness

I Introduction

Five of the eight books in this unit are written by people who
have specialized in the applied field of clinical psychology.
Four are actively engaged in helping those people to change
who society variously calls the *handicapped*, the *mentally ill*,
the *maladjusted* and so forth. The fifth has turned his attention to the world of advertising and market research. Because
of this training bias, it is worth talking about how such people
see themselves in order to try and understand why radical
views are to be found within the clinical field far more often
than in any other branch of psychology.

II *The role of the clinical psychologist*

There are three major areas into which psychologists have in-
filtrated and set up shop to apply their discipline – education,
industry, and psychiatry. The first thing you do when you
have set up shop is decide exactly what you are going to sell
and then put a board up outside stating clearly what your
wares are and inviting all who are interested to come in and
sample them.

Of course, there are often many teething problems to start with. You may not be selling precisely the wares the buyer wants. You may be too familiar or too standoffish in your demeanour. But in the end, if you are successful, you will have a thriving business with satisfied customers.

Just so your applied psychologist encounters problems in establishing a professional role for himself. But in education and industry the problems can be described as superficial rather than fundamental. In education the psychologist can use his carefully learned scientific language and conceptual system if he should so wish. He may decide that this language and viewpoint is irrelevant to the understanding and helping of children. But if he changes the language he does so because HE wants to and not because such a change is forced upon him. He can continue to work, think and, to a reasonable extent, talk in terms of ideas from developmental psychology. He can use concepts from various theoretical frameworks such as those of Piaget (see C2). Or he can use notions about the effects of maternal deprivation on the subsequent psychological development of the child, or notions from social psychology about how we repeatedly impose society's rules of behaviour on successive generations of children (see C1, C3).

Likewise, in industrial psychology, a theory of motivation can be applied to explain absenteeism or Freudian theory used to interpret the results of depth interviews in market research. (See E1, E6, respectively.)

Of course, both educational and industrial psychologists may find they have to translate some of their jargon into a language understandable by the teacher or the director whose company has commissioned the investigation of the best way to sell his product. But for the clinical psychologist entering the field of psychiatry the position is very different.

First and foremost he has to work within a conceptual framework that is totally foreign to him and at times diametrically *opposed* to his professional conceptual framework. He has to work within a para-medical setting and use a para-medical language which has been devised to maintain the parallel with general medicine (which the outlook of the medically trained psychiatrist often seems to require). So this shop-keeper cannot sell the wares he thinks he is best fitted to sell nor describe his shop and his goods in words that come naturally to him. It is therefore perhaps not surprising that the great majority of non-medical models of 'man-in-need-of-adjustment' are suggested by clinical (non-medical) psychologists.

III The notion of norms

But who decides that something is wrong and therefore needs changing? It is society – our society. It says that *this* type of behaviour is acceptable and *that* is not. And the standard against which *this* and *that* is judged is a *norm*. You are a part of a norm and I am a part of a norm. Or, to be more precise, we are a part of a multitude of norms. I think we are deluding ourselves if we cherish the conception of being unique individuals each doing our own 'thing'.

A norm is a standard – usually in your head – against which you compare something or someone. We are not concerned here with the normative standards of the specific sections of society to which each of us belongs – such as whether it is desirable to put the milk into tea first or last; say '*pardon*' or '*what*'; confess to having wicked thoughts about Jews or keep them hidden. Either form of behaviour may be 'correct' in certain settings. What is 'wicked' is determined by the norms or required behaviours of the group to which we wish to belong.

These sorts of standards are, in some sense, voluntary. We can and do periodically change our allegiance but the standards of society only change if many people show their wish to do things differently. We do not all want to behave whimsically but, if we do, we do so in the clear knowledge that our whimsicality will be apparent. For how can we be deviant if we do not know what being 'normal' is?

IV Normal and abnormal

If normal is defined as being something that is expected or usual then it should be possible for an encyclopaedia of norms to be concocted for all mankind. Many attempts have indeed been made to do just this in specific areas, such as the books on etiquette popular in the 1920s and 1930s for those who aspired to join the socially élite. They had their cookbooks for manners as well as for food. But there are two disadvantages to such cookbooks. First, there is the basic inherent difficulty that there is a very wide variety of ways of doing things normally. It is normal to wipe your nose rather than let it drip, but there are an enormous number of ways in which 'wiping' can be accomplished.

A second disadvantage to the cookbook system is that it is the enemy of change. If things are put into print we come to believe that they are 'true', in the sense that if we want to belong to a particular group then there are certain ways of behaving that are 'right'. The changing of the soccer rule to allow in substitutes was a mammoth task indeed. But where there is a range of acceptable behaviours, change can occur imperceptibly and without revolution. When norms are too rigidly adhered to it suggests that they may have become too important to the individuals concerned. The rules have been invested with meaning which gives them the function of life-support systems. The threat implicit in the possibility of change is discussed in Chapter 7.

Every group spells out, explicitly or implicitly, what it considers to be normal and what abnormal; what abnormalities it is prepared to tolerate and what it will take steps to eliminate. Very closely linked with the normal–abnormal dichotomy is that of good–bad. Society usually sees what is normal as being 'desirable' and what is abnormal as 'undesirable'.

61

Thus the concept of handicap (undesirable) is intimately related to the norms and values of the group or culture to which the person belongs. Rosemary Shakespeare (see F2) points out that a person deemed handicapped in our fast-moving, industrial society, might not be so called in a farming community; that a person is more likely to be called handicapped in an urban than in a rural community, or if the person is a boy or man rather than a girl or woman (it is easier to keep girls at home in a protected environment where they can be given jobs around the house).

The social rules also dictate whether there will be pressure to keep a child or adult at home or have him segregated. At the present time there is a social pressure to have those children or adults designated as handicapped because of a low level of intellectual ability sent to special institutional units. But the opposite pressure will be applied to a family to keep someone who is very severely physically handicapped at home. These expected behaviours often have a very strong moral tone. It is wicked, lazy, selfish, for one individual not to sacrifice his life for another. Not that this is often the case, but it can happen. And most often it is the sacrifice of the woman's life for the man's. The woman gives up her job to look after her disabled husband – or tries to be both worker and nurse. The point at issue is not whether her decision to give up her job and the development of her own self is right, or her decision to get someone else to look after her husband is wrong. But rather that it should be a personal decision and not dictated by the norms of a society.

Probably no one deals more directly with the norms or expectations of behaviour than the advertiser. Through his market researcher he has to find out just how to present his product to a particular group. If it is a middle-class product like an after-dinner mint, then the people in the advertisement have to act precisely as a middle-class family would be expected to behave (only perhaps a little more so). Many a product has died an unnatural death because the 'product positioning' was wrong and the advertisement offended some group norm.

But there is another use of the word *norm*. Psychologists talk a great deal about *normative data*. For instance, in order to make a diagnosis in medicine it is necessary to know what the expected range of blood pressures is in normal people under normal conditions. To get this information an investigation has to be carried out testing the blood pressures of many people. Sampling is obviously important as they will have to be representative of different age and occupational groups and so forth. You will find this dividing up of population referred to as 'market segmentation' in the consumer world (F6).

But there is one other factor to be considered. The majority of people have holes in their teeth. Is this therefore normal? The majority of children bite their nails or wet their beds after they are supposedly toilet trained. Is this therefore normal? What is healthy and what is unhealthy?

V Models of illness

How remarkable it is that people respond to illness throughout the world in such very different ways. Just like responses to pain, it seems as if response to illness is determined by the society in which we live. We learn how to be ill and how to play the doctor/patient game. The child reacts to not feeling well by staying quiet. He has to be taught to go to bed and to accept the principle that others know better than he what is good for him. Kelly (1966) has commented that we, in the Western world, have carried this to extremes now. We no longer think we should deal with our own psychological problems, we go and lie down to be treated for them.

The idea of illness, as with other concepts, varies according to where one is standing. It can be a condition, a role, or a process, depending on whether one has a medical, sociological or psychological bias. From a medical perspective one talks of a process; from the sociological standpoint there is talk of status with rights and obligations; and from a psychological perspective illness is an experience which affects both the person concerned and those around him. But through the ages mankind has changed the ways in which it has conceptualized the states of good and bad health.

a) *The supernatural model*

For centuries illness was regarded as some force or 'being' that attacked poor, passive, undefended man. The witch doctor or some other being with special power would be called in to try and locate in which part of the body the foreign invader had settled. Having located the spot, his job would be to drive it out by magical and ritualistic practices.

With social and religious changes in the Middle Ages came the notion that illness was the result of sin. It was a form of punishment of sin for which one had to atone. Germs were then discovered and in time it was possible to see them through the microscope. When the evil could be seen, people came to think in terms of war. The body was 'invaded'; it had 'defences'. Hence today we use such metaphors as 'he is putting up a good fight' or 'he is resisting the infection'.

b) *The medical model*

It was Hippocrates who put medicine on the map. He had no patience with the idea that disease was a punishment sent by God. He emphasized that it is a morally neutral event caused by attacking organisms against which man can defend himself.

c) *The environmental model*

Ecologists stress that the occurrence of illness depends both upon man's heredity and upon the present and past effects of his environment. Great emphasis is placed on man's inherited disposition to respond in a certain way. This is not an alternative to the medical model, but rather an extension of it. Its stressing of predisposition helps to explain why people react differently to *apparently* the same set of circumstances and *vice versa*.

d) *A psychological model*

The psychoanalysts talk of 'escape into illness'. The cause of an illness is therefore to be sought in the individual. The question that has to be asked is 'from what personal problems is he escaping?' Illness is not seen as caused but motivated. Balint (1957) has analysed the medical consultation and describes the 'offerings' of the patient. These represent his conflicts and his attempts to escape from them. Balint sees the doctor as being the commonest form of medicine in Western medical practice.

Another psychoanalytic concept often called into use is that of *denial*. The patient is said to 'deny' when he does not see the full implications of his complaint. He denies because to see his complaint as the physician sees it would cause him too much anxiety. It is a form of self-defence. From another point of view it could, of course, be said that maybe the situation is *not* as serious seen through the patients' eyes as it is seen through the eyes of the medical practitioner. But as was discussed in Chapter I, Freud's man is a passive creature at the mercy of unconscious mechanics and to see denial from the denier's viewpoint involves a radical turn-about.

But the importance of this psychological approach for us here is that the psychoanalytic theory of Freud led inexorably to the notion of psychosomatic illness. There are now so many theories to account for the supposed psychological origin of many disorders that it has been suggested that our society may be changing to a self-blaming conception of illness after many years of the guilt-free germ theories. We, each one of us, feel responsible for allowing ourselves to get so tensed up that we 'give ourselves' gastric ulcers; for driving through traffic in crowded towns and so allowing our blood pressure to soar and our heart rate to increase. Balint considers that the person participates in the development of his own illness. Many of us have now been made to feel responsible for our health – it is a part of us – and feel guilty for allowing our health to suffer. We are guilty, not for having caught an illness, but for having lost our health.

e) *The social model*
Sociologists view illness as an impairment of capacity to perform one's social roles. Illness is a form of deviance which affects society. It is not of interest because of its causation but because of its actual occurrence or incidence – it is a problem to be solved and not a result of something. In society's attempt to control this type of deviant behaviour it creates roles to be played.

Whenever groups of people form, there is an expectation widely shared by its members of what *should be* the behaviour of people occupying certain positions. What a typical occupant of a given position is expected to do constitutes the *role* associated with that position (see B2).

In this definition a role can be seen as encompassing, among other things, the duties, obligations and rights of the position. The rights of a position are defined in part by the roles of related positions. For example, rights of the doctor are defined in part by the roles of the patient and nurse. The patient follows orders, while the nurse carries them out.

Thus roles are interdependent. For example, the traditional role of the general practitioner included the expectation that he would have an intimate and friendly interest in the patient as a person and *vice versa*. But the role of the medical specialist is defined primarily in terms of impersonal expertise.

Kelly (1955) sees roles as being defined in terms of expectancies but he takes it a step nearer the person. For him, a role exists between two people when one attempts to see the situation through the other's eyes. When you, as patient, attempt to look at yourself through the eyes of your doctor (however difficult this may sometimes be) you are playing a role in relation to your doctor. This does not mean you have to agree with him. You may conclude that he sees you as 'a nervous stomach'. If that were the case, you might not try to make him understand the particular stress you are under at the moment. But you still are an active participant in the relationship.

The sick man is thus seen as having a role in society just as the well man has. And the role corresponds closely to medical expectation. The sick man behaves in certain ways. He is exempted from his well-role responsibilities. Even though he may be responsible for his illness because of negligence, he is not expected to cure himself.

There is no one way of defining illness. It would seem that the medical, environmental, psychological and social perspectives must all be taken into account when we, in the Western world, try to conceptualize 'illness'.

VI Models of wellness and the concept of mental health

Have those who subscribe to a particular definition of illness succeeded in defining wellness? Most medical definitions imply that health is the absence of disease. They define it in terms of physical, mental, and social 'well-being'. But with these definitions it is not possible to be a 'little' ill or 'reasonably well' or just 'so-so'.

Jahoda (1958) suggests we look at health and disease as if they are two dimensions so that everyone has 'sick' aspects and 'well' aspects at any point in time. She gives an example of a visitor in a psychiatric hospital who said 'There's nothing wrong with him except he thinks he's Napoleon Bonaparte'.

Most of us probably have a pretty good idea of what we mean by 'peak wellness' and by 'death'. But it is now clear things are not as straightforward as they seem. Watson (1974) argues that there is not a simple dichotomy between life and death. He argues that there are degrees of death – you can be a little bit dead or a lot dead. The stage beyond death is what he calls 'goth'. This is when cells cease to have a pattern or organization that is characteristic of their group or species. It seems we do indeed live in a time of change – when many of our seemingly most stable concepts are being called into question. Whether we find this exciting, alarming or stupid depends on how we see our world.

Any discussion of mental health must necessarily lean heavily on Jahoda's *Current Concepts of Positive Mental Health* (1958). In this book she has analysed the various definitions that have been suggested and offers her own solution to the problem. 'What problem?' you may rightfully ask. Well, first Jahoda points to the fact that there are at least two ways of defining the concept of mental health. One is to classify individuals as more or less healthy and see this as a relatively enduring aspect of their personality. The other method concentrates on actions at some particular moment in time. She then points to a third way in which the concept is *used*, as when people talk of a society or group being sick or healthy. This is a mistake. Mental health must relate to a living organism with mental faculties. All a society can be is conducive to healthy or unhealthy behaviour.

Jahoda then discusses three unsatisfactory ways of defining positive mental health. The first is based on a definition of the *absence of mental illness*. Apart from the fact that the concept of mental disease is itself difficult to define, human behaviour must be considered in conjunction with society's norms and values. A mental symptom cannot be viewed in isolation.

Another way of defining mental health is in terms of *normality*. In this definition one is again mirroring definitions of physical health and illness, but with even more difficulties emerging. Anthropologists have provided a wealth of information showing the tremendous flexibility of human behaviour and the wide range of behaviours that are tolerated as normal in one culture and are regarded as abnormal in another.

Once again though, there is more than one way in which the word 'normal' is used. A person can be normal in that he behaves as society says he should. In this case there is no difference between this and the concept of mental health. So to define mental health in terms of a synonym is not going to get anyone anywhere very quickly. Another way of defining normality is in statistical terms. The things the majority do are normal and hence the things the minority do are abnormal. But do we really mean this?

The distribution of intelligence test scores are normally distributed. That is, most people get scores between 85 and 115 and increasingly fewer get scores higher than 115 and lower than 85. But Shakespeare (F2) talks of those at the lower end as being 'handicapped' and they are indeed abnormal since there are relatively few of them. But surely we must therefore talk of those few at the top end of the scale as also being handicapped and abnormal. Of course, we do not do so. Society brings in a value judgment about what is good and what is bad. To be very high in measured intelligence is 'good' and to be very low is 'bad'. Statistical normality is thus no use to us in defining positive mental health.

A third attempt at definition is in terms of *states of well-being*. But to say a person is mentally healthy if he is functioning well socially and feels good is all right provided we are prepared to say that the mentally unhealthy person is one who is unhappy, and functioning poorly socially. But whether he is unhappy because of particular distressing social or personal circumstances or because he is always 'like that' must surely be important; however, this definition takes no account of that fact.

Having dismissed absence of mental illness, normality and well-being as satisfactory ways of defining mental health, Jahoda looks at five other criteria. A popular way of talking about positive mental health is in terms of the *self*. In order to be considered mentally healthy, we must be able to introspect about ourselves, be aware of what we are doing and why. Maslow is quoted as saying:

> Our healthy individuals find it possible to accept themselves and their own nature without chagrin or complaint or, for that matter, even without thinking about the matter very much.
>
> They can accept their own human nature with all its discrepancies from the ideal image without feeling real concern. It would convey the wrong impression to say that they are self-satisfied. What we must rather say is that they can take the frailties and sins, weaknesses and evils of human nature in the same unquestioning spirit that one takes or accepts the characteristics of nature. (1950:16)

Maslow's ideas are also important in another criterion of mental health which is concerned with the growth, development and *self-actualization* of the person (see D2). Maslow focuses on the motivational aspects of self-actualization. Growth motivation (as distinct from deficiency motivation which leads us to satisfy our needs) leads us to realize our potential capacities and talents. And the more of this type of motivation the individual possesses the healthier he is.

Some authors use as a criterion the *integration* of all processes and attributes of the individual as a definition of mental health. The psychoanalysts focus on the balance between the three parts of the personality, id, ego and superego.

Still others look to see how individuals *cope with stress*. It is generally accepted that anxiety is found in the healthy as well as the unhealthy. If we can cope with it without disintegrating, then we satisfy this criterion of mental health.

If we can make our own decisions we satisfy yet another criterion, that of *autonomy*. Are you independent? If so you satisfy Maslow, who thinks autonomous people are those who get their chief satisfactions from within themselves and do not have to rely on other people or the world outside.

There are those who say to be mentally healthy we have to

see the world as it really is. But who is to say what the world is 'really' like? If each one of us 'sees' a situation in terms of our own set of interpretative concepts may we not all be equally right? Teacher calls a child lazy. But another teacher observes that the child is always active and keen in the gymnasium. Who is right? Of course they both are. They are simply looking at different aspects of the child.

To avoid this problem with what is 'correct' perception, Jahoda suggests using 'relative freedom from need-distortion'. This does not mean 'that needs and motives are eliminated; nor that they have no function in perception. The requirement is of a different nature: the mentally healthy person will *test* reality for its degree of correspondence to his wishes or fears. One lacking in mental health will assume such correspondence without testing.' (1958:50) In our perception of ourselves and others, we may have particular difficulties but to be mentally healthy we must at least treat the other person as worthy of our concern.

Lastly, we come to *environmental mastery* as a criterion of mental health. This refers principally to the ability to love; to be adequate in love, work and play; to be satisfactory in our interpersonal relations; and to have a capacity for adaptation and adjustment.

After discussing all these criteria which are unsatisfactory in themselves, Jahoda suggests we stop looking for the one and only criterion of mental health. In particular she stresses the need for research. We should stop increasing the concepts and criteria and start producing some facts so that the useful criteria can be sorted out from the not useful.

Even if some satisfactory definition of mental health is eventually arrived at, where does it get us? It obviously gets us doing something about it – promoting it – making us all better, healthier people. Society's value judgement comes in here. To be mentally healthy is 'good'. But Jahoda asks 'Good for what? Good in terms of middle class ethics? Good for democracy? For the continuation of the social *status quo*?

For the individual's happiness? For mankind? For survival? For the development of the species? For art and creativity? For the encouragement of genius or of mediocrity and conformity?' (1958:77) These questions are of vital importance and your answers are as good as mine.

4
Mad, sad or just plain bad

Society has its deviants sorted into four neat packages. There are those who are sufficiently unintelligent to be called *subnormal* (see F2); those who are sufficiently physically incapacitated to be called *handicapped* (also F2); there are those who are sufficiently wicked to be called *criminals* or *anti-social*; and those who are sufficiently psychologically disturbed to be called *mentally ill* (see F3).

There are naturally overlaps between these broad categories of deviants. A criminal can be physically or mentally handicapped. A subnormal person can commit a crime and so be put in the overlap category of the *mentally abnormal offender*. Since no institution acknowledges that they own such a person, he often gets shuffled from prison to hospital and back again, like some pathetic human yo-yo. But here we are concerned with those society says are 'ill' and are therefore not responsible for their state or actions.

I Models of psychological deviants

a) The religious model
Just as theorists have models of men so societies have models of deviants. For many centuries people who were deviant in

psychological ways were dealt with in a very similar manner to those with physical complaints. The supernatural model was used and the person with the 'power' to put things right was considered to be in touch with those who controlled us poor mortals. The devil or evil spirit was ousted or the punishment administered and the person returned to conforming to society's norms or died or carried on as before.

The notion that people who flouted the norms of society were either wicked or possessed resulted in many terrible 'treatments' such as burning at the stake, whipping, or maiming. It must never be forgotten that our model or theory of deviance dictates our 'treatment' of the deviant.

b) *The medical model*
Its general implications. When medicine took over the mental deviants, the devil and his ilk were put to flight. These deviants were now *sick*. The concept of mental illness evolved in the belief that it could be the spitting image of its physical counterpart – or the poor relation at least. Concepts of physical medicine are applied to those whose behaviour is in some way psychologically deviant and who are held not to be responsible for that behaviour. They are *ill*, and those who take responsibility for their care are called *psychiatrists*. In addition, the concept of mental illness has implications and ramifications that permeate the whole of society and dictate the way in which people who have psychological problems are dealt with. Thus, the behaviour is called *pathological* and is classified in terms of *symptoms* which lead to the making of a *diagnosis*. The process whereby the deviant behaviour is changed or whereby the person is helped to make a readjustment so that he can conform again to society's norms is *treatment*, either physical or *psychotherapeutic*. The deviant is cared for and treated in a *hospital*, is there as a *patient* and, if the treatment is successful, is said to be *cured*. This is the dominant model in the mental hospital; it is a medical model

which sees patients suffering from disease entities even though these may be little understood.

No elaborated conception of 'normality' is involved here. There is no theory of normal functioning from which these patients deviate. It is rather generally assumed that common sense tells one how to differentiate between the 'normal' and the 'ill'. But it has been suggested in Chapter 3 that these two concepts are difficult to define as entities let alone be distinguished with ease. If the illnesses are not well understood, it stands to reason that the majority of treatments cannot be derived from any clear formulation of the illness. Electroconvulsive therapy and drug treatments are used because they are thought to have been proved useful both in practice and on the basis of clinical research and not because they are based on a viable theory of the way in which they function.

The mental disease concept. At the risk of labouring the point to death, it is worth looking at the concept of disease as used in psychiatry, as disease is what clinical psychologists so often help in diagnosing. As an example, let us take the most common mental 'disease' diagnosed in the Western world – schizophrenia. People with this disease are said to account for the occupation of up to 25 per cent of the hospital beds in Britain, so it is something worth consideration. It is called a 'functional' disorder because no evidence exists that there is any physical cause for the abnormal behaviour. Many psychiatrists are convinced that this is simply because people have not looked in the right place with the right techniques in the right way at the right time.

So, while the search for a cause goes on, filling thousands of journal pages with 'findings' in the process, the psychiatric fraternity makes do with diagnosing the disease by the presence of certain types of overt behaviour. And here the problem gets complicated. There are a number of specific symptoms or abnormalities of behaviour that, given enough of them, results in having the diagnostic label 'schizophrenic' stuck on. But Bannister (1968) has pointed out the disjunctive nature of the concept. Say there are ten symptoms in all that come under the heading 'schizophrenia'. One schizophrenic may have symptoms one to five that earn him his label while another gets his stripes by having symptoms six to ten. They can have the same label and yet have no abnormalities of behaviour in common. Guertin has remarked:

> The desire to bring schizophrenia into the realm of clearly defined disease entities is a noble one; but unfortunately, investigators engaged in the task resemble dogs chasing their own tails ... It is generally agreed that schizophrenia is such an inclusive label that there is no single behaviour symptom always present in every patient, nor does a group of schizophrenics show much uniformity in traits or symptoms. (1961:200)

Treatment. It is usual for a model or theory to have clear implications for treatment. But not so in psychiatry, as Bannister, Salmon, and Leiberman (1964) showed. They statistically analysed the relationship between diagnosis and treatment in 1,000 cases. The results were not clearcut either for or against a relationship existing. The authors suggest that there are variables other than diagnosis that may be equally important in deciding on a particular treatment.

The model within which one works may not fully determine the sort of 'treatment' one metes out, but it does affect the sort of research that is done and the relationship that will exist between those who confront each other when they attempt to iron out psychological problems.

Research. Research within the medical model must of necessity be concerned with some of the following: the identification of disease entities; the investigation into whether Brand X or Brand Y drugs will produce the superior result; and the tie-up between symptoms such as anxiety with the underlying physiology. Such research is clearly useful. If one is going to prescribe drugs at the current rate, it is vitally important to prescribe the best one for dealing with the symptom and the one that will produce the minimum in side-effects. But the point is that these are not the *only* questions that can be asked. Other models lead to the asking of different questions which in turn leads to different ways of going about things.

Therapeutic relationship. The relationship in 'talking' or psychological treatments, as opposed to physical treatments, must be that between *doctor* and *patient*. The basic ingredient of this is dependence. The patient (patiently) awaits relief of his symptoms at the hands of the person who is the expert. Maybe this is the best relationship if the treatment is the use of drugs – there is nothing for the patient to do but wait for the drugs to 'work'. The occupational therapist might keep the person busy; the social worker might ensure that the person has a job to go to when 'cured'; the.psychologist might give some tests to quantify the expected change in some way; but it will be the drugs that do the 'real' work. In this context there is no need for any other type of relationship. But maybe some other relationship is required when there is only 'talking' involved.

Clinical psychologists. It is difficult to overemphasize the dominance of this medical conceptual framework in the field of psychiatry with its central concept that of *mental illness*. But this is meaningless from the point of view of psychology as a science. There is nothing whatever in the training of a psychologist that leads him to think in these terms. Yet it is the key concept of those with whom he must closely work. It is a concept about which he must learn if there is not to be a total breakdown of communication. The medical model can be taken to imply that the clinical psychologist is basically a medical technician who carries out tests as required by the doctor; rather in the manner of the operator of an electroencephalogram, or X-ray or pathology laboratory technician.

The term 'psychometrician' is used to describe the psychologist who measures psychological variables in a certain way. It seems designed to underline some sort of equivalence with other 'measurers'. However, the parallel is clearly a poor one in that the pathologist who carries out a blood analysis is working in terms of the same physiological concepts that are used by the physician, and their work is thereby integrated. The psychologist who administers an intelligence or personality test is working in entirely different terms from the psychiatrist and some kind of translation has to take place so that the end-product is described in the language of psychiatric diagnoses and symptoms.

In essence such a model is obviously of a very different kind to the various models operating in general psychology, such as the 'personality' model (which can envisage behaviour as socially maladaptive) or some model of a psychological process which places the individual at an extreme point on the continuum. Such models cannot separate out particular behaviours as constituting 'illness'. In this sense Freudian, Skinnerian, Kellyian models are all examples of psychological and not medical models.

The use of a psychological model carries with it the implication that the psychiatrist is a medical man functioning as an untrained psychologist while the medical model implies that the psychologist is a technical auxiliary who provides evidence which the doctor takes into account in arriving at a diagnosis. But some psychologists do fulfil this role and devote a considerable amount of time to applying psychological tests to give answers to questions that are phrased largely in 'medical' terms. For example, the question might be 'Is this person suffering from brain damage?' or 'Does this patient show evidence of schizophrenic thought disorder?' But even here, the tests will give answers in non-medical language. They will be in terms of such things as I.Q., psychological traits, or construct relationships. It is important to realize that not only is there translation of the answers, it is obvious that quite often questions are being reframed as well.

It is the medical model itself that has largely been responsible for the clinical psychologist's failure to fulfil the role allotted to him many years ago – that of psychometrician. There is, of course, the translation problem. But over and above that the psychologist has been required to measure such grossly inadequately defined concepts as 'brain damage', 'schizophrenic thought disorder', 'personality'. And with the diagnostic tests, the problem has basically been one of standardization. To construct a test one has first of all to select a sample, or samples, of people who are known to have the 'thing' to be measured. But, just as not all psychiatrists agree about the definition of schizophrenia, so they do not all agree as to what sorts of behaviours jointly constitute the disorder of thinking that is characteristic of some schizophrenics. Thus the test for diagnosing the presence or absence of this symptom can be no better than the diagnostic abilities of the psychiatrists concerned.

It is really a most interesting situation in which psychiatrist and psychologist collude. The psychiatrist has a concept, ill-defined, which he calls schizophrenic thought disorder. Along come the clinical psychologists who design a test to tell the psychiatrist what he already knows – but less accurately since the test results and psychiatric opinion never agree 100 per cent. The argument is that not all psychiatrists have sufficiently long experience to enable them to be confident in their diagnostic ability and the patients are not always clearcut members of a particular diagnostic grouping. So maybe the test does better than the inexperienced psychiatrist with the person who does not clearly show the particular disorder.

The one area in which the clinical psychologist has clearly severed the connection with the medical model is the area of handicap. The child born with a limited capacity to adapt to changes in its environment is only in need of medical care when it contracts some physical illness. Otherwise, its needs are for assessment of its existing abilities, for attempts at analysing how these abilities can best be utilized, and assistance in developing to the full as an individual.

It may seem petty and childish for clinical psychologists to bite the hand that feeds them. But some consider they now have sufficient bodies of knowledge and techniques for helping those with psychological problems to be allowed their freedom to see what they can do. This means they are no longer content to be helpmeets of psychiatrists (helpmeets without a place in the power structure). They are now in competition with the medical profession. Not all clinical psychologists feel this way of course, but a substantial enough number do for them to be given a hearing.

However, it is by no means only psychologists who increasingly raise their voices against the monopoly of the medical model. In fact, much of the present controversy surrounding it is due to the writings of the sociologist Goffman and the psychiatrists Szasz (1961) and Laing (1967) (see particularly F8 for detailed coverage). The medical model can be seen to have many direct effects on the patient. He is classified as *ill*. This means that he is able to relinquish his social responsibilities. If he commits a crime he is 'guilty but insane'. He is often taken out of the community and placed in a new total social environment called a mental hospital.

Goffman gives his views from the sociologists' standpoint in 'The Medical Model and Mental Hospitalization: some notes on the vicissitudes of the tinkering trades' (in *Asylums*, 1968). He, like the psychologists, points out the fallacy of seeing emotional problems in the same light as medical ones. He offers instead the 'tinkering model':

The type of social relationship I will consider in this paper is one where some persons (clients) place themselves in the hands of other persons (servers). Ideally, the client brings to this relationship respect for the server's technical competence and trust that he will use it ethically; he also brings gratitude and a fee. On the other side, the server brings: an esoteric and empirically effective competence, and a willingness to place it at the client's disposal; professional discretion; a voluntary circumspection, leading him to exhibit a disciplined unconcern with the client's other affairs or even (in the last analysis) with why the client should want the service in the first place; and, finally, an unservile civility. This, then, is the tinkering service. (1968:285)

But his most condemning piece is in the early part of his book *Asylums* in which he describes how he sees the career of the mental patient the moment he is first labelled 'mentally ill'. He sees the mental hospital as a 'total institution', one in which there is a barrier to social contact with the outside world and a barrier of some kind to departure. He describes what he calls the 'degradation ritual' that takes place on admittance in which the patient is made to see just how different from and inferior to the staff he is. Then comes the authoritarian approach and a description of the fact that rigid routines militate against individuality. He sees the patients getting into a conflict situation, having to decide whether to leave hospital as quickly as possible or to conform to the pressures and so give up the struggle to remain a *person*.

Although Goffman writes of mental hospitals in the United States of America, much of what he says is applicable to many British mental hospitals. For those who no longer have visitors to bring in clothing and other 'personal' articles, there is a uniformity of dress, of hair cut, of response to the voice of authority and, perhaps the most clearly depersonalizing condescension of all – the ubiquitous 'dear'.

What does the recipient/client/patient think of the medical model and the mental hospital? The 1974 October issue of the magazine *Mind Out* reported the results of an inquiry into mental care in Britain from the point of view of those on the receiving end. Taken at its face value, it makes horrific reading:

> The empty tranquillized faces queuing for their daily drugs seem to sum up in my mind the current state of treatment of mental illness in many of today's mental hospitals.
>
> As an outpatient in one of London's teaching hospitals it was normal to wait 1-2 hours after the appointed time. Eventually, quite often, patients waiting for the consultant would be told he would not be attending that day. Two hours of waiting when one was in a nervous state and a journey of $1\frac{1}{2}$ hours home.
>
> The only thing my stay in a psychiatric ward did for me was to make it abundantly clear that the only person who would be able to solve my problems was me.

It was, of course, not all bad. But most of what was said by the recipients of mental treatment was not much of an exaggeration. Much comment was related to the problem of not being treated as a person but rather as someone with an illness which seemed to make them incapable of communicating in a comprehensible or responsible way.

> ... he summoned the courage to ask his psychiatrist a question that was very important to him. The psychiatrist ignored the question and asked him why he carried two biros in his top pocket. R.C. would very much have welcomed the chance to talk more fully about his problems. But an interview with a doctor often takes place only once in three months and lasts only a few minutes. 'Rather pointless questions like the date or some simple sum in arithmetic are asked (as if the mentally and emotionally disturbed were also mentally deficient!)'

A short time ago a book presenting the case *for* the medical model was published. It is called *Models of Madness and Models of Medicine*. In it the authors, Siegler and Osmond (1974), attack those who try and deprive the patient of his medical rights. The mental patient should be allowed the sick role and his family has the right to be given 'a concise diagnosis of their relative's distress'.

The authors recognize that there may be no wholly satisfactory treatment for the 'illness' but think the physician can carry out certain 'time-honoured moves' to reduce the suffering of family and of the sufferer. They rightly point out that one of the best ways to reduce anxiety about something is to give that 'something' a name. But in the case of mental illness, where there is no certainty about the nature of such illness, this comes close to a confidence trick or magic. But apart from conferring a name on the deviant, the doctor can re-assure the sufferer and his family that the patient is not suffering from something worse and he can reassure both that what is happening is a natural occurrence and that no one is to blame for it. But for Siegler and Osmond, the physician can now 'exercise his authority, he can confer the sick role on patients, which places them within the medical model of illness.' (Siegler and Osmond, 1974:71)

There seems to be something rather circular in that argument, especially when the authors agree that they have no proof that schizophrenia, for instance, is a disease entity. But they condemn others for treating sick patients without proof of the nature of the disorder:

> There is no convincing evidence that traumas during early childhood play much part in causing schizophrenia, as psychoanalysts and other proponents of the family model believe. Therapists who oust mental patients from the sick role and place them in psychoanalysis do so with the best intentions. Although analysis has done little or nothing for schizophrenics, its proponents *seem unaware that the theory is wrong*. (italics added)

Siegler and Osmond go on to say:

> Once again, a consensus is developing that schizophrenia is a genetic-biochemical illness. *If this proves to be correct,*

it will not be enough to say to those parents' families who have been stigmatized with accusations of driving their children mad, 'We are sorry. We made a mistake.' (italics added) (1974:78)

Would it not be reasonable to add that, if schizophrenia turns out *not* to be a genetic-biochemical illness, and the deviant has been shut away in a mental hospital for twenty years and been tranquillized up to the eye-balls, it will not be enough to say 'We are sorry. We made a mistake.'?

Surely, where there is doubt there should be room for anyone who has serious proposals for the reduction of suffering to put them into practice? It is just such alternative approaches that the medical model attempts to restrict. It is difficult for those 'without' not to see those 'within' the safe walls of the medical model as operating a closed shop policy.

c) *The moral model*

One of the clearest underlying assumptions of the concept of mental illness is that the person is not responsible for his deviant behaviour. If society (or doctors) thought he were, then he would be sent to prison rather than 'treated' for his misdemeanours. Szasz has argued that the concept of mental illness is a myth. Historically, many ideas to explain the inexplicable have been seen, not as theories, but as self-evident causes of the events; for example, concepts of witches, instincts, and gods. Szasz thinks that mental illness is a myth in that sense and has outlived its usefulness.

He points to the basic assumption that some abnormality of the brain makes people ill in *just the same way* that a person with a malfunctioning liver is ill. In this he sees two fundamental errors. First, a belief, false or otherwise, cannot be explained by a defect or disease of the nervous system in the way that, say, a perceptual defect can. Second, the error is epistemological, that is:

it consists of interpreting communications about ourselves

84

and the world around us as symptoms of neurological functioning. This is an error not in observation or reasoning, but rather in the organization and expression of knowledge. In the present case, the error lies in making a dualism between mental and physical symptoms, a dualism that is a habit of speech and not the result of known observations. (1960:114)

As an example, he gives the fact that the medical practitioner looks for signs (e.g. fever) and symptoms (e.g. pain) in physical illness, whereas he looks to the patient's descriptions of himself and his world for the mental symptoms. The statement 'I am Napoleon' will be judged a symptom depending on whether the medical practitioner believes him or not. The medical practitioner compares the statement with his *own* beliefs and with his *own* interpretation of the norms of the society in which he lives.

Szasz tries to describe the norm from which the mentally ill are thought to deviate and finds it has to be stated in psychological, ethical, and legal terms. But the remedy to the deviant's behaviour is sought in terms of *medical* measures.

Who then defines the norms and hence the deviation? Szasz offers two answers. In the first case, it is the person himself who decides he deviates sufficiently from his own norms and (or) those of society and so seeks help on his own account. In the second case, it is someone other than the deviant person, perhaps a relative, doctor, or society itself, who calls in a psychiatrist. All this creates a situation in which deviations described in psychosocial, ethical, or legal terms are 'corrected' by medical methods. This, Szasz argues, is logically absurd:

I submit that the idea of mental illness is now being put to work to obscure certain difficulties that at present may be inherent − not that they need to be unmodifiable − in the social intercourse of persons. If this is true, the concept functions as a disguise: instead of calling attention to con-

85

flicting human needs, aspirations, and values, the concept of mental illness provides an amoral and impersonal 'thing' – an 'illness'. We may recall in this connection that not so long ago it was devils and witches that were responsible for man's problems in living. The belief in mental illness, as something other than man's trouble in getting along with his fellow man, is the proper heir to the belief in demonology and witchcraft. Mental illness thus exists or is 'real' in exactly the same sense in which witches existed or were 'real'. (1960: 116)

Szasz's alternative model is that man is not mentally ill but has *problems in living*. These problems are the consequences of living in a highly complex society. We should all work toward solving the problems of human relationships and we can do this rationally. For finding the problems of living more overwhelming than most, the person should not be taken out of society and put into a mental hospital. The social reality of such action is still today what it was centuries ago 'punishment without trial, imprisonment without time limit, and stigmatization without hope of redress.' (Szasz 1969: 57)

Of particular relevance at the moment is the discussion concerning the possible misuse of psychiatry for political ends. In 1972, Shaw and two colleagues reported on their assessment of the stifling of political dissent by the misuse of psychiatric diagnosis in the USSR. After analysing the available evidence from six examples, they reached:

the inescapable conclusion ... that Soviet psychiatry is being used for political ends. Political dissenters, often very articulate, are being quietly removed from an active role in society, with minimum fuss and publicity, to be placed in a mental institution. Presumably this practice occurs because it is the one legally sanctioned situation where the 'patient' has no rights whatsoever, and in which he may be detained indefinitely without right of appeal. And the law sets no limit to the duration of 'treatment'. (Shaw *et al*, 1972: 261)

It is Szasz's view that such incarceration without recourse to the law is a crime against humanity. Has he a point? Is it just possible that in North America or in Europe politicians could get hold of a friendly psychiatrist and have a troublesome opponent involuntarily committed? Certainly both countries have expressed their concern about the possible happenings in the Soviet Union.

Another person who focuses on moral issues is Mowrer (1960). He is particularly concerned about what the 'illness model' does for man's perception of himself in relation to his life. From the individual's point of view, to have something mentally wrong with one is 'living death'. He feels guilty. It is morally sinful. Here the issue is much broader than whether deviant behaviour for which the individual is not held responsible should be called a disease or not, it concerns beliefs of the moral nature of human life.

But even if one accepts that the mental illness model enables society to deprive a person of his legal rights without recourse to law, and thereby it is morally demeaning, at the moment it offers no alternative way of investigating and explaining this type of deviant behaviour. Mowrer comments that perhaps 'our best policy is to become frankly agnostic for the time being, to admit that we know next to nothing about either the cause or correction of psychopathology and therefore ought to concentrate on *research*.' (quoted in Maher, 1966 : 31) Exactly what form this research should take is still not clear.

d) *Statistical model*
This is a category proposed by Maher (1966) to describe the work of such people as Eysenck (see D3). These people have been concerned to identify patterns of behaviour that can be reliably described. These patterns are established by the factor analysis of data obtained (see p. 52). As Maher points out, this is an approach rather than a model. Nothing is involved except an attempt to describe certain patterns of

behaviour, to measure these, and then to classify them by means of statistical procedures. It is therefore different from the other categories in which the process underlying the deviant's behaviour is seen in terms of 'disease', or 'morality'.

In the dimensional approach no specific process is seen as underlying the disorder of behaviour. It is simply a statistical statement of what people do, and is described in relation to dimensions of personality (i.e. measures) rather than in terms of classification. The personality dimensions in Fig. 4.1 are those of extraversion and neuroticism. And people showing identifiable forms of deviant behaviour can be located along these two dimensions. For example, someone with a high score on neuroticism and introversion would, in the two-

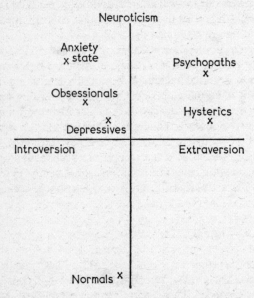

Fig. 4.1 *Position of one normal and six neurotic groups in two-dimensional framework determined by canonical variate analysis of objective test performances (Redrawn from Eysenck, 1960)*

dimensional space, appear like those traditionally classified as suffering from an anxiety were they to be overcome by problems of living.

e) *Comment*

The various models of deviance have far-reaching implications. The medical model is the presently accepted model for viewing psychological deviance. It is from this background that much of radical psychology has stemmed. But it is not the only impetus. Other 'red rags' come from what the various models of man lead practitioners to do in an effort to bring about change in people.

You will have noticed that there has been no mention of specific theoretical models such as the Freudian, Skinnerian or Kellyian. Each of these has clear implications for changing people and they are treated separately in the following chapters. But first there must be a discussion of another concept – a central one in psychological change – *psychotherapy*.

5
Change and the dynamic model

I Introduction

Before discussing Freud's contribution to psychotherapeutic practice, it is necessary to clarify what we mean by the term *psychotherapeutic*.

We have all, at one time or another, wanted to change aspects of ourselves and at other times (or even at the same time) have wanted to change aspects of others. For centuries such change was most often brought about within the context of religious experience, and in Eastern cultures this is still the case. But the Western world, as it steadily turned from religion and increased its emphasis on science, developed 'specialists' (sometimes self-professed) in the changing business. The tide has turned full circle so that now religious practitioners go to professional, 'scientific' changers to be taught how to help their parishioners – they come out of such training as *pastoral* psychologists.

In his book *Psychotherapy East and West*, Alan Watts discusses the considerable similarities between Eastern thinking and ways of life and Western psychotherapy. The main resemblance being 'in the concern of both with bringing about changes in consciousness, changes in our ways of feeling our own existence and our relation to human society and the natural world'. (1973:13)

At the present time, Western psychology is becoming increasingly fascinated by ideas and procedures that have been known to the Eastern mystics for centuries. This is that the mind has the power to control the body. *Biofeedback* techniques, as they have been aptly named (see A2), enable a person with, say, high blood pressure to lower it without drugs, with only the power of the mind. What psychologists have not yet shown any sign of doing is studying Eastern literature to see how such relationships are conceptualized. But biofeedback, as we know it, is in its early days and here the concern is with the 'talking' methods for bringing about psychological change.

Extraordinary as it may seem, there was virtually no psychotherapy as we know it today before the beginning of this century. When people talk of psychotherapy, they most often think, if they know anything at all about it, of psychoanalysis in some form or other. The psychoanalytic procedure as described by Freud is based on the idea of 'uncovering' repressed impulses and forgotten ideas which will lead to insight and thus improvement of the symptoms. It is not really surprising that psychotherapy is regarded as a synonym for psychoanalysis since Freud was the first explicitly to describe a theory and method for bringing about change in people by getting them to talk. It is the general rule operating here that the name of the 'first' is always given to the second and third and so on *ad infinitum*, irrespective of the fact that these followers may well bear little relationship to the original. For instance, how many people still call a carpet-sweeper a 'Hoover' in spite of the fact that it may be made by a competitor.

For the layman psychotherapy still tends to be shrouded in mystery and so produces unease. Unease in its turn often leads to humour, so the psychiatrist becomes the 'head-shrinker' even though he may more typically give his patients drugs. To the layman, psychologist and psychiatrist are alike in being 'able to read the mind'. Thus, in most people's minds, the psychiatrist and psychologist are thought of as principally in the psychotherapy business.

In America particularly, psychotherapy is a very saleable commodity. In some special gatherings it is quite usual, even mandatory, to discuss one's latest psychotherapy session. It is by no means necessary to be 'ill' before one goes and lies down to be treated for one's problems.

The early psychotherapists such as Freud, Jung, and Adler were medical men who each had a theory of personality which not only explained human nature but described how the theory could be applied to help people who were seen as behaving in socially deviant ways.

Since then, however, the vast majority of new forms of therapeutic procedures have come from psychologists rather than medically trained people. For example, there are those who extended Skinner's operant conditioning procedures for use in the consulting room, or there is Kelly who created an entirely new psychology of man which is equally at home in helping us understand the person who society views as normal or abnormal. A notable exception to the above is Wolpe, a psychiatrist, who developed desensitization from classical conditioning principles (see A3 and F3).

Of course, if psychoanalysis had worked, there would have been no need for the development of new methods and theories. But it certainly does not work so well that everyone is satisfied. Even Freud himself thought it was an interim procedure to be used until biochemical measures were perfected. Not only are there doubts about the effectiveness of psychoanalysis, but the method involves a long hard struggle. The person may have to attend for treatment several times a week for several years.

There are several battles going on today involving psychologists. One is between non-medical clinical psychologists and the medical profession (usually psychiatrists); one between exponents of various forms of psychotherapy, in which category we will here include behaviour therapy; and one within the whole field of psychology between descendants of Locke and Kant. The so-called radical movement in psychology had its roots in the clinic in general and in psychotherapy in particular. There are at least two reasons why rebellion affecting the whole of psychology should have found some of its most vociferous supporters among clinical rather than other groups of psychologists. One is a desperate attempt to escape from the strait-jacket of the medical framework. But the other is perhaps less obvious. There is no other group of psychologists which has such direct contact and involvement with individual persons than that comprising those involved in some form of psychotherapy. There really can be few more inspiring activities than the commitment of oneself to helping another get out of his present personal predicament.

II Definition

But first, what is this psychotherapy we are talking about? Surprising though it may seem, there is no one generally acceptable definition of psychotherapy and the psychotherapist. Perhaps there is wisdom in this seeming madness. For to define is to set limits. It means that some *practices* would be included within its confines and others excluded. It means that some *people* would be recognized as being able to carry out these practices and others be *persona non grata*. It leads to *professionalism* which is discussed more fully in F4.

The basic argument against professionalism is that, by saying one has particular skills, one gains social status and the right to accept money for the sale of those skills. This in turn gives power over others and thus can be used to oppress in the name of society. In relation to professionalism in psychotherapy, one opinion is:

Some 'good' therapists do help people, putting them in touch with themselves and their political reality, but of course so do other 'good' people, untrained as therapists. Thus, there is no 'good' skill that being a therapist confers; and where 'good' skill exists, nothing that makes it the exclusive property of therapists. Even to label an ability to deal with human problems as a skill, removing it from the realm of ordinary human accomplishments, is adding to the mystification. It is one of the maddening facts of our time that people believe themselves incapable of dealing with the most ordinary human conflicts without the aid of a 'specialist'. (Henley and Brown, 1974:61)

The lack of a commonly agreed definition is not necessarily a bad thing in itself.

There can be no doubt that the demand for 'talking treatments' is enormous – and seemingly increasing. Is it really so necessary or is the whole populace being fooled?

In his article 'Detherapizing Society', Kunnes considers this to indeed be the case and more:

Therapy has the effect of imposing consumer standards. The consumer-patient aspires to the emotional life and social life style of the therapist. It is difficult to go beyond the therapeutic-consumer society unless we understand that therapy inevitably reproduces such a society, regardless of the nature of the therapy ... The existence of therapists and therapy, in part, produces demand for it. Once we have learned to need therapy, all our activities tend to take the shape of client relationships to other specialized institutions. (1974:21)

But if we assume that some people do reap some benefit from some psychotherapy, then the ultimate question must be 'What type of approach helps what type of person?'. This question is a long way from being answered.

Let us look at the definition given in the dictionary of

psychological and psychoanalytical terms (English and English 1958). These authors define psychotherapy as:

> the use of any psychological technique in the treatment of mental disorder or maladjustment. The term is very general. It includes 'faith cure', suggestion, hypnosis, psychoanalysis, provision of rest, assurance, advice, consultation designed to relieve anxiety, psychodrama etc. Nearly always personal consultation is a part of the technique, sometimes the whole of it. The term carries no implication about the seriousness of a disorder ... the duration or intensity of treatment, or the theoretical orientation of the therapist. But the term should be reserved for treatment by a professionally trained person – i.e. by a clinical psychologist, psychiatrist, or psychiatrist social worker. (1958: 429)

This type of definition relates the procedure to the *practitioner* and is fairly liberal in its scope. As you might guess, many definitions proposed by psychiatrists limit the term to the 'form of treatment in psychiatry in which the psychiatrist, by his scientific thinking and understanding, attempts to change the thinking and feeling of people who are suffering from distorted mental or emotional processes'. (Polatin and Philtine, 1949)

Most definitions though are in terms of *theoretical* (explicit or implicit) goals. Thus, Freud saw psychoanalysis as a means whereby patients could be led to have 'insight' into why they had become psychologically ill in the first place. Likewise Kelly says 'Our view of the ultimate concern of clinical psychology as a discipline, and our notion of *therapy*, is that of a psychological process which changes one's outlook on some aspect of life ... the psychological reconstruction of life.' (1955: 187)

Another group of definitions focuses on the *relationship*. Freud placed great importance on the development of the relationship within the therapeutic setting, it was a means to an end which was the gaining of insight. For Rogers there is something in psychotherapy that is beyond words: 'It is a process, a thing-in-itself, an experience, a relationship, a dynamic ... Therapy is the essence of life ...' (1951), and '... therapy has to do with the *relationship*, and has relatively little to do with techniques or with theory and ideology.' (1962)

But not all definitions come from such examples of specific therapeutic approaches. For instance, Haley has the interesting notion that people have symptoms, not because they are ill, but because they have come to use them as tactics in human relations. So for him, successful therapy is a process whereby a therapist maintains control of what kind of relationship he will have with a patient. (1963:19)

Before moving on, a few words about words. 'Client' or 'patient'? The suggested change is a byproduct of the medical model rebellion. Just as Kelly wanted to swap the word 're-construction' for 'therapy', so 'client' was swapped for 'patient'. Not a very satisfactory alternative, but the best that has been thought of up to now.

The professional therapist can be seen as having a political part to play in society. He is required to help society's deviants adjust to society's norms. If society is against homosexuals then they are deemed 'sick' and so can be 'treated' and are 'cured' when their faces light up in the presence of members of the opposite sex. All therapists must, therefore, at some time during their professional lives, ponder deeply on the ethical problems involved in what they are doing. Is he to help a person *change* or is he to help him to *adjust*? (see F8).

While it is generally agreed that chatting to one another can bring about change (for good or ill), there is no general consensus of opinion as to what should be chatted about; who should talk to whom; and what the relationship between the participants should be. So let us now look at the content of the various approaches, at the therapeutic relationship and at some of the implications of the various methods.

III Freud

Medicine, of itself, has no words of wisdom to give the psychiatrist who wants to embark on one of the most exciting of human endeavours – that of helping another human being change.

If a psychiatrist holds a view that psychologically disturbed man is suffering from something other than a physically-based disorder, the psychological model he is most likely to work within will resemble Freudian or dynamic theory. Although Freud was medically qualified and practised medicine for a number of years, his theory is clearly a psychological rather than a medical one.

It is the common practice among non-psychoanalytic psychologists to regard most Freudian concepts as being outside their professional frame of reference, yet many clearly use them at a personal level. But apart from this dual-standard often adopted, there is another reason why these concepts should be given due consideration by the clinical psychologist. The majority of the psychiatrists with whom the clinical psychologist will work will think and work using Freudian conceptual terms. Thus, for any reasonable communication to take place, the psychologist should have at least a passing acquaintance with the main theoretical concepts (see D3).

It must be made quite clear that there are by now many, many variations of Freudian theory and of psychodynamic therapeutic procedures. But throughout this volume, Freud's views in their more 'pure' form have been discussed since he was, after all, the first.

Even though Freud's theory is basically psychological rather than medical, he never gave up stressing the importance of biological factors as determinants of human behaviour. The dualistic nature of his theory is clearly seen in his view of the hysterical symptoms that were so important for his whole theory and practice of treatment – *psychoanalysis* (see F3).

a) *A theory of the deviant*

Deviant behaviour is not seen by the psychoanalyst as the result of some 'illness' but as the blocking of expression of the psychic energy system. Freud came in contact with many patients who had symptoms of, for example, paralysis of an arm. But the paralysis described paid no heed to the known anatomy of the nervous system. Rather, the patient would describe the paralysis in terms of the popular conception of how the nervous system works. This was a *conversion* symptom. A girl might have the feeling that her parents were making too much of her younger brother – he is allowed to lead a free and easy life while she has to stay at home and look after her invalid mother. She suddenly finds she cannot use her arm – it is paralysed. She has translated (or converted) a purely mental phenomenon into a physical disorder. A symptom is thus seen as a communication to the environment from the unconscious. But although Freud constantly keeps this dualistic view of man before us, it is clear that it is *mind* that matters and that the only real connection between the mind and body is through the instincts.

Nearly all of man's neurotic difficulties stem from the sexual instinct. This is virtually synonymous with *libido*, the only source of energy in the mind. It is this concept of mental energy that earns the theory its name 'dynamic'. This emphasis on the notion of mental energy is a major difference between this approach and that of the behaviourists and the phenomenologists. When this energy is blocked in its passage from the unconscious to the conscious mind, trouble starts. Repression occurs and, for Freud, this is 'the corner-stone on which the whole structure of psychoanalysis rests.' (1957:16)

When life becomes too much of a problem for a person he takes 'flight into illness'. This has the primary advantage of saving the person from any further psychic effort and the secondary advantage that others who are important in the person's life are upset and may be changed as a result of the illness. Freud compared neurosis to a monastery. It is a place of refuge where people can go when they feel too weak to face more of life's frustrations.

It is thus no good treating the girl's paralysed arm, because the reasons for it are to be found in the hidden (repressed) meaning the symptom has for her. This can be brought about by her gaining insight into what brought the illness about.

b) *Method for producing change*

The basic method used in psychoanalysis is *free association*. In this the patient is encouraged to say whatever comes into her head, no matter how silly or embarrassing it may be. The typical psychoanalytic setting is to have the patient lie on a couch with the therapist sitting behind her head out of sight. The posture resulted partly because Freud thought it would be disruptive to the patient's free association activity to have feedback from the therapist's face, but also because Freud admitted that he could not stand the thought of being stared at for up to eight hours a day! Freud was a 'reluctant therapist' in that he had larger goals in mind than those of producing insight in mixed-up people. He wanted to create a theory that would account for the behaviour and experiences of all people and not just the deviant.

For Freud, the neurotic was far from being free. For him, 'the child is truly father to the man'. He is locked into his part like a character in a play. The patterns of behaviour developed in childhood are re-enacted in adulthood. In this sense he is determined. His behavioural patterns are frozen. But by insight he is enabled to redirect the course of his life.

It is very difficult to test the assumption that insight is necessary for change. For if the person changes without insight, it can be argued that perhaps he has not *really* changed. If, on the other hand, there is insight galore but no change, it can be argued that the insight is not the 'right' insight or else it is still not sufficiently *deep*.

c) *The relationship*

In psychoanalysis, the therapeutic relationship is all-important. Any psychological change is seen to take place because of the childlike dependence that is fostered in the patient. It is fostered in several ways. The therapist has initial superiority in that the person comes to him for help. Also, almost inevitably in psychoanalysis, the patient makes a heavy financial investment in the enterprise and may even be made to hand over the money each week. But the greatest of 'Freud's ploys' is the placing of the patient so that he is virtually lying at the analyst's feet – or at least lying below him in space. From this position the analyst can watch the patient but the patient cannot watch the analyst. In addition, the analyst is superior in that he has all the answers while the patient only has an 'unconscious'. Anything the patient says can be interpreted by the analyst to suggest that what the patient *said* is not what he *meant*.

This childlike dependency is fostered so that the patient can re-enact some troublesome aspects of his infantile past. Thus the therapist is treated as if he were someone in the patient's past life – *transference* has occurred. The goal is thus to provide a certain type of relationship and thereby to learn something of the patient's past history.

Haley makes a thorough analysis of the strategies the psychoanalyst adopts in order to maintain his 'one-up' position. For instance:

> Perhaps the most powerful weapon in the analyst's arsenal is the use of silence. This falls in the category of 'helpless' or 'refusal to battle' ploys. It is impossible to win a contest with a helpless opponent since if you win you have won nothing. Each blow you strike is unreturned so that all you can feel is guilt for having struck while at the same time experiencing the uneasy suspicion that the helplessness is calculated. (1963 : 94)

Part of the training analysis is designed to enable the

would-be analyst to develop ways of counteracting the patient's desperate attempts to get 'one-up' on him.

The relationship in psychoanalysis is thus one in which there is an all-seeing, all-knowing master who deals skilfully with the patient as he desperately struggles in a childlike fashion to come to grips with his master and to overthrow him.

d) Extension

One of the spin-offs from psychoanalysis is the use of free association in market research interviews (see F6).

In market research the aim of free association in the *depth interview* is to allow the person's mind to wander freely around the desired topic:

in the hope that it may throw light on the respondent's motivations, feelings, attitudes, and prejudices with regard to a particular problem, such as his use of toothpaste or his habits with regard to cheese. The main difference therefore, between the clinical interview carried out by a psychologist and a depth interview carried out for market research purposes is that the former is individual-based while the second is problem-based. (Berent, 1966)

Whether one agrees or not with the individual/problem difference as stated is of no import. What is of concern is the extent to which the data obtained are 'true' reflections of what a person (or group of people) had in mind. It is important who does the interpreting of the respondent's responses in all such interviews.

In the psychoanalytic situation, it is the therapist who interprets the content of the patient's mental meanderings within the confines of psychoanalytic theory. The rules of interpretation are laid down. In the depth interview, it is highly unlikely that any two interviewees will come up with the same idea expressed in the same words. Thus, to obtain any generalizable results, interpretations have to be made.

Some people are of the opinion that depth interview information should lead only to new ideas concerning the product and that these should then be tested out in another study using a greater number of people. Numbers used in depth interviews tend to be small, since having to have one interviewer to one respondent makes it an expensive enterprise.

Another spin-off from psychoanalytic theory is the notion of the *phallic symbol*. Apart from free association as a pathway to the unconscious, Freud made extensive use of dreams. His book *The Interpretation of Dreams* is not only generally regarded to be his greatest work, but to be one of the great classics of our time. The dream is an expression of a repressed wish and so the message has to be disguised and distorted. This is the price to be paid for the unconscious (repressed) material being allowed to enter consciousness:

> The more striking and for both sexes the more interesting component of the genitals, the male organ, finds symbolic substitutes in the first instance in things that resemble it in shape – things, accordingly, that are long and upstanding ... further, in objects which share with the thing they represent the characteristics of penetrating into the body, and injuring – thus, sharp *weapons* of every kind, *knives*, *daggers* ... In the anxiety dreams of girls, being followed by a man with a knife or a fire-arm plays a large part. This is perhaps the commonest instance of dream-symbolism ... The female genitals are symbolically represented by all such objects as share their characteristics of enclosing a hollow space which can take something into itself; by *pits*, *cavities* and *hollows* ... (Freud, 1953 : 154)

Some advertisers argue that it is possible to reach the unconscious by a sort of reverse-dream symbolism procedure. They use sexual symbolism in advertisements. For example, once upon a time there was a petrol advertisement on television. A young girl and a man spring lightly into a long, low, thin, sports car. Oh, the power of the engine as it growls and thrusts the long thin car up a hill overlooking a most magnificent blue Mediterranean Sea! Up the hill this powerful car winds until it comes suddenly to a halt at a petrol station. Out jump the young couple from the door (away from the camera) and disappear from sight – presumably a little way down the hill. But our attention is now riveted on the petrol pump – it nearly fills the whole TV screen. Slowly and steadily it points down towards the open petrol tank – a black circular hollow. The petrol pump enters the hollow. After a few moments, the petrol pump is withdrawn and the young couple reappear, jump into the car, and streak off into the blue. A knowledge of Freud's sexual symbolism adds a new dimension to television advertisements!

But it is arguable whether, if we are in ignorance of such things, we unconsciously recognize the symbols. Do they indeed encourage us to buy the articles advertised?

e) *Come the rebellion*

The usual criticism levelled against Freudian psychoanalysis is that its basic concepts are untestable and its efficacy has failed to be demonstrated. And the evidence on which these criticisms are based is discussed in F3. Freud stated that 'psychoanalysis is a method of research, an impartial instrument, like the infinitesimal calculus, as it were.' (1961:36) This means that you have an idea about the cause of a symptom, you deal with that cause as a result of which the symptom disappears. Your theory is validated and the whole thing is internally consistent. This is often called the 'coherence theory of truth' as opposed to the 'correspondence theory of truth' usually adopted by experimentalists. In the latter case, one tests a hypothesis against events that are independent of the procedure from which the hypothesis was originally derived. One question concerning Freud's scientific method concerns how one can be sure that what the patient recounts concerning his childhood actually happened. 'Is it not possible that the Oedipus complex is merely the distortion of childhood relationships made by an adult who has sexualized his recall?' (Rychlak, 1974:226)

One of the great problems with psychoanalytic theory is that Freud was constantly changing his theory throughout his life and this makes criticism very difficult. But Jahoda has said that 'Freud survives for two reasons: he used several complex and logically distinct principles of explanation and he did not mind being inconsistent.' (1972:271)

Untestable? Unstable? So be it. But there is yet another criticism that says Freud is wrong in his basic conceptualization of man. Freud conceived of man in isolation – he can be understood in his own right and not in relation to his environment. Insight is gained when the patient sees the situation as the therapist thinks he should. Resistance in therapy is overcome when the patient gives up the unequal struggle of resisting the analyst. In both these cases, the traditional interpretation is that the unconscious is resisting the probes of the analyst and that unconscious conflicts have at last to be made conscious. But from a Marxist standpoint, the unconscious has worked as a device for obscuring the politics of therapy. 'The unconscious is used to obscure the power relations between people by locating the dynamics and issues of intersubjective life inside the individual.' (Brooks, 1973: 344) If a woman is unhappy in her marriage her analyst may tell her that it is because of unresolved unconscious conflict concerning her feelings for her father. But many, including Marxists, might say it is to do with the social reality of the world outside.

Freud is also held accountable, partially at least, for the notion of male supremacy. Of course, this idea was prevalent for centuries before the present, but the argument is that Freud certainly gave men another three inches on their heels and so increased the height from which to look down on their lesser brethren. One inch for *penis envy*, one for the *vaginal orgasm*, and one for the *masculinity complex*.

In brief, penis envy is what it says. The girl is envious of

104

the little boy's penis – she feels she has been castrated and blames her mother for this – (obviously her mother has been a bit careless too).

To develop normal sexuality, the female must transfer sexual sensitivity from the clitoris to the vagina and henceforth have orgasms centred on the penetration of the vagina. If she insists on retaining pleasurable sensitivity from stimulation of the clitoris she is demonstrating a masculinity complex since the clitoris is a rudimentary penis. So goes the Freudian view. Throughout his writings one finds reference by Freud to the inferiority of women. To give but one example:

> You know, too, that women in general are said to suffer from 'physiological feeble-mindedness' – that is, from a lesser intelligence than men. The fact itself is disputable and its interpretation doubtful, but one argument in favour of this intellectual atrophy being of a secondary nature is that women labour under the harshness of an early prohibition against turning their thoughts to what would most have interested them – namely, the problem of sexual life. (Freud, 1964:79)

Thus, amongst other things, Freud is held responsible for hindering the advance of psychology (or at least persuading some to deviate from the true path of science); for failing to live up to the dreams of Marxists; and for being partly responsible for the low status of women in the eyes of the rest of the world – Men. (For a full account of the theory, see D3, of the treatment procedure, F3, and of the radical view, F8.)

6
Change and behaviour

I Introduction

The behaviourist model has been extremely important in the development of the clinical psychologists' increased confidence. For the first time they were able to turn to a sizeable body of literature concerning normal human behaviour to explain deviant behaviour without having to resort at all to medical concepts.

In behavioural terms, the deviant is either someone who has been unlucky enough to have someone louse up the time-tabling of his reinforcements or else has had his gut reactions cemented to a specific situation which then swells like a balloon until it fills the person's living space penning him in the corner so that he cannot escape. (See A3 for descriptions of operant and classical conditioning.) In the behavioural model, as in the medical model and the dynamic model, the deviant is not held responsible for his deviance. It is not his genes that are at fault, nor his psychic energy system, but he is now seen as having learned maladaptive responses.

Like all models, this one has its limitations. It is best at explaining fairly specific deviations of the more *neurotic* type. It finds far more difficulty in accounting for so-called *psychotic* behaviour such as that found in schizophrenia or manic depression (see F3). But that should not be held against the behavioural model makers as they are still alive and kicking and could well extend the range of applicability of their procedures.

II Behavioural psychoanalysis

Two men, Dollard and Millar, can be regarded as transitional figures in therapeutic history in that they had experience with psychoanalysis, and later concluded that man is essentially a product of learning, particularly emphasizing the principle of reinforcement. (This is empirically defined as any event that increases the probability of a particular response occurring again in a similar situation. It can be positive – in the case of food, or negative – in the case of pain.)

a) The theory of the deviant
Basically, Dollard and Miller see the neurotic as being driven to do something; this arouses anxiety which, in turn, drives him *not* to do that thing. In this sense the neurotic is *stupid* (not intellectually of course). Because of this approach–avoidance behavioural conflict, the person increasingly becomes miserable. The conflict is unconscious and is due to previous *repression*. In this case repression is the 'automatic tendency to stop thinking and avoid remembering.' (1950:220) They have thus neatly translated a psychoanalytic concept into behavioural language. The consequence of stopping thinking about something unpalatable is that no verbal labels become attached to the thought.

The neurotic is stupid in that, with no labels with which to identify the problem, he tends to generalize from old responses to new situations. A person with a rejecting father might respond to all authority figures in adulthood as he did to his father. He 'acts out' this previously learned pattern of behaviour in an inappropriate way. It is this 'acting out'

107

behaviour that is the symptom of neurosis or psychosis. These symptoms do not solve the basic conflict in which the neurotic person is plunged, but they tend to reduce it and so, in part, succeed. 'When a successful symptom occurs it is reinforced because it reduces neurotic misery. The symptom is thus learned as a habit.' (1950: 15)

b) *Method for producing readjustment*
Since the neurotic behaviour is learned, it can be unlearned and new habits formed. Psychotherapy provides the conditions in which a) these habits can be examined, identified, and unlearned – this is the 'talking phase' – and b) new and more rewarding patterns of behaviour can be acquired – the 'performing phase'. The neurotic has to learn verbal labels for his unconscious conflicts so that he can look at them in the cold light of reason. Apart from applying new labels, he can relabel and by so doing see some of his past behaviour patterns in a new light.

There is also considerable similarity here between psychoanalysis and the approach of Dollard and Miller in the use of 'insight' (see p. 99). They provide an almost straightforward translation of the Freudian concept into stimulus-response language. If the therapist's interpretation of the patient's utterings (i.e. suggesting a more appropriate verbal label) gives the patient a new 'insight' into his problems, then this greatly increases the probability of behavioural change. The patient can learn this procedure by imitating the therapist and it then comes to have the characteristics of a drive. The patient can continue the process on his own. 'In some cases the patient will know immediately that he has created a valuable new sentence because drive reduction (insight) occurs at once.' (1950: 299) But one major difference is that Dollard and Miller do not demand that the insight be in the therapist's terms. Rather, the insight is in the person's own terms.

Another difference is that they do not see the gaining of insight as a necessary condition of cure. Rychlak considers that this change in the way insight is conceptualized is of vital importance in the historical advance of psychotherapeutic procedures. Delving into the patient's past is not now useful in itself, its use lies in enabling the person to compare past and present events and to see that they are, in fact, different. Insight thus serves as a means for bringing about change:

> It is this highly pragmatic view of 'insight' as a kind of instrumentality in the therapeutic process, which make Dollard and Miller the *bridge theorists* to the behavioural theories ... (of Skinner and Wolpe). Though still cloaked in the older terminology of therapist interpretation and client insight, theirs is a new vision in the history of psychotherapy. Change comes about in the present, and no matter what one *says* about why the initial or resultant patterns of behaviour array themselves as they do, the processes of change have a relevance all their own. (Rychlak, 1974:321)

The next step in the changing view of insight was to stop looking into the person's past altogether and to concentrate on what is happening in the present.

c) *The relationship*

The relationship is considerably different from the one-up/one-down relationship in classical psychoanalysis. Dollard and Miller stress the collaboration between therapist and patient. They are both responsible for 'cure'. The patient must work hard and the therapist will do his best to help the patient verbalize his past, and deal with his emotions, and the general caring attitude will support the patient in his struggle *with himself* rather than with the therapist.

III *The behavioural psychotherapy of B. F. Skinner*

With the behaviour theorists 'in pure culture' came the entire dropping of the past, the focus being directed to the here and now. Another change was to emphasize action rather than talk.

a) *Theory of the deviant*
The person applying *behaviour modification* in the classic sense has no interest in the past of the person and sees no need for insights. The maladaptive behaviour (symptom) has been learned and so can be unlearned or removed by manipulating present reinforcements.

b) *Method of treatment*
To take a very simple example: a patient persistently comes into the Ward Sister's office uninvited – much to the annoyance of Sister. This undesired behaviour has to be *extinguished* and the desired behaviour *reinforced*. An analysis of the situation reveals that every time Mrs. Brown comes into Sister's office uninvited, Sister gets out of her chair and, with a few well-chosen words, leads Mrs. Brown to a seat in the ward. Having established what is the undesired and what the desired behaviour, things can proceed. To extinguish the undesired behaviour Sister must pay *no attention whatever* when Mrs. Brown comes into her office. Hard though this may be, we will assume that eventually Mrs. Brown gets tired of the exercise and goes back into the ward and sits down. Now Sister gets up and goes into the ward and pays attention to Mrs. Brown, thus reinforcing the desired behaviour. Assuming that the analysis is correct and that the reinforcer is 'attention', Sister should have no more trouble (for various procedures based on this theme, see principally F3).

One aspect of this approach relates to the medical model discussion. Behaviour therapists argue forcibly that once designated as sick or mentally ill, the patient will assume that role. If he is a 'good' patient, he will give up all attempts to exert his individuality. He will be a passive and malleable patient. But this very behaviour is counterproductive for therapy. Very often it is considered necessary to give the patient training in self-assertiveness, particularly if he has been in hospital for some time. But this can lead to bad feeling between the psychologist and ward staff resulting in confusion for the patient.

One of the applications of the operant approach is the so-called 'token economy' situation. A ward of patients is treated like a giant Skinner box. This is a box designed by Skinner in which an animal can escape or obtain some positive reinforcement by pressing a lever or pecking at a button (see A3). An analysis of the situation is made, the behaviours to be altered noted and the reinforcers for each patient determined. Then, each patient is given a token every time he behaves in the desired way. With these tokens the patient can 'buy' his cigarettes, his food, his television programme, and so forth (see F3).

c) *Extensions*

Skinnerian conditioning has been applied to another aspect of psychotherapy. The concepts have been used to explain what is actually happening in the 'talking' therapies. The 'insight' in psychoanalysis is seen as resulting from the therapist having selectively reinforced certain of his patient's responses. He has 'shaped' the behaviour by reinforcing responses that are closer and closer approximations to what the therapist perceives as the ultimate desirable conclusion. But not only is the patient being conditioned by the therapist's 'Ums' and 'Ahs' but the therapist himself is conditioned to behave in this way because of his many years of personal analysis.

It was Greenspoon in 1954 who started off this 'social reinforcement machine' concept of the psychotherapist. All Greenspoon did was to get a person to say all the words that came into his head for about ten minutes. These words were then analysed into grammatical classes (nouns, verbs, and so forth). The 'therapist' then selected, say, verbs, as the class of words to be reinforced. Thus, every time the 'patient' used a verb in conversation, there would be a 'mmm' or an 'I see' or some other noncommittal response from the 'therapist'. Having got a count of the number of verbs used in the patient's non-structured speech, it was an easy job to see whether the proportion of verbs had increased with the specific reinforcement. They had.

If this had been the only study one would not need to pay too much attention to it as there were a number of weaknesses in the design, such as whether it is reasonable to consider that 'saying words that come into one's head' is the same thing as 'speaking meaningfully'. But there have been many variations on the Greenspoon theme and they all suggest the same thing, that it is possible to change the way a person speaks by selectively reinforcing aspects of his speech.

The operant approach is therefore completely different from dynamic approaches, both in the ways in which man is conceptualized and in the supposed reasons for change occurring. For the behaviourist it is *doing something* to a person that changes his behaviour rather than the achieving of new 'insights' into his own behaviour. The Skinnerian methods are nicely summed up in the phrase 'behavioural engineering' – mental mechanics *par excellence*.

Another influential person in the behavioural psychotherapy field is Joseph Wolpe (1969).

IV *Joseph Wolpe and reciprocal inhibition*

a) *Theory of the deviant*

Like Freud, Wolpe had a medical training but, unlike Freud, he practised medicine, working as a psychiatrist. His study of the work of Pavlov led him to develop a behavioural approach to treatment that focuses on the classical conditioning of bodily emotional (autonomic) responses to an environmental event (see A3). Wolpe took anxiety as his core concept, particularly concerning himself with the bodily sensations that emotion arouses (see A2). If something happens to make the person anxious while eating potatoes, the feeling of being 'full' 'attaches' itself to the feelings of anxiety. This may result in the person experiencing anxiety whenever he begins to feel full of food. This, it is argued, could lead in time to the person avoiding food altogether.

b) *Method of treatment*

In behaviour therapy the approach to cure is to reintroduce the person, gradually, to the thought of, or actually, being full of food. To start with the person gives a detailed account of everything related to the problem – and many things that, at first sight, may seem unrelated. For instance, a person who gets very anxious when going into a large office may, in fact, be afraid of people in authority. A detailed analysis is made of the situations that are likely to lead to anxiety; ranging from no reaction at all to those that produce the response in its greatest intensity. The development of this *hierarchy* of anxiety-producing situations is essential to the procedure of *systematic desensitization*.

If the person complains of fear of going out and about, then the treatment procedure would be to systematically desensitize the person to the outdoors. One way of doing this is to first teach the person the skill of relaxation. This is not as simple as it may sound and it may take several sessions before the person can relax deeply at will. The person is then instructed to think about (visualize) the situation that is first in the hierarchy of anxiety-producing situations; that is, one that produces virtually no anxiety. The argument is that the act of relaxing is incompatible with the feeling of anxiety – the one response *reciprocally inhibits* the other. The person moves quickly on to the situation that comes second on the hierarchy and thinks about it until he is able to report no anxiety being experienced. The procedure continues in this way until the person is able to think about the most previously anxiety-producing situation with now no fear.

Wolpe found that many of his patients were not well able to express emotions even though they may be overwhelmed by anxiety from within. For this sort of person he advocated *assertive training*. While this can mean learning how to express aggressive feelings in a socially acceptable way, it can also mean being able to say one is afraid, pleased, or just plain bored. These procedures can be used along with a systematic desensitization programme.

A technique for which Wolpe was not directly responsible, but which makes use of the reciprocal inhibition method, is *aversion therapy*. In this, some unpleasant sensation (e.g. nausea) is induced in the person every time he indulges in the undesired behaviour or an electric shock may be given. The person gives up the undesired behaviour because of the unpleasant associations. This technique has been used, for instance, in treatment of homosexuality and other sexual 'perversions'. In these cases, the person may be given a substance to produce nausea before being shown nude figures of his sexual preference, or else be given an electric shock while actually looking at the pictures. He might also be reinforced for looking at a person of the opposite sex in various states of undress by pleasurable experiences induced by injections of sex hormones.

One of the arguments against the behavioural engineers and behaviour therapists is that it is no use treating the symptom, one has to treat the cause. This of course stems from the Freudian idea of unconscious conflicts being the root cause of neurotic behaviour. But the argument continues that if one does not deal with the root cause, then other symptoms will appear to *compensate* for that which is lost. The behavioural therapists have been at pains to show that such *symptom substitution* does not necessarily take place. And if it does, rarely according to Rachman, 1971, then reasons can be found to account for it. But there is still some way to go before it is possible for these scientists to predict when symptom substitution will and when it will not be a problem.

a) *Theory of the deviant and method of treatment*

Stampfl uses the term *implosion* to describe his therapeutic technique – a 'bursting inwards' as compared with an explosion or bursting outwards. He feels that the person may be full of emotion and may show it but acts upon it at a verbal level only.

The approach is similar to Wolpe's systematic desensitization in that hierarchies of feared situations are constructed. But with implosion there are two types of situational cues that are thought to trigger off avoidance responses. There are those that the patient is aware of and which are usually directly related to the symptoms and there are those higher up the hierarchy, 'sequential cues', which are thought to be more related to the original cause of the problem. These latter cues may be psychodynamic, such as conflicts to do with sex or aggression, and may only become apparent during treatment.

In addition to this reversion to interest in the past, Stampfl retains many of Freud's concepts. For instance, the reason why neurotic symptoms are retained is that they take the mind off even more terrible thoughts – mostly repressed ones. That is to say, the person has forgotten what originally made him anxious and one of the purposes of treatment is to get him to remember. Thus, if the person is afraid of going into crowded places and is made to think of exactly that, he will not only be flooded with emotion but will be in a better position to discover more and more about what it is all really related to. 'The fundamental hypothesis is that a sufficient condition for the extinction of anxiety is to re-present, reinstate, or symbolically reproduce the stimuli (cues) to which the anxiety response has been conditioned, in the absence of primary reinforcement.' (Stampfl and Levis, 1967: 498)

Stampfl is thus in the tradition of Dollard and Miller in using specific learning theory notions but retaining many of Freud's concepts.

The behaviourists, like the psychoanalysts, see man as essentially a determined creature. But in psychoanalytic theory man's behaviour is also *directed* by his unconscious psychological processes, whereas the behaviour of the behaviourist's man is blindly determined by the 'laws of nature', that is by what the environment does *to* him during the course of his life. His behaviour has been *shown* to be manipulable by external events without his being aware of anything happening.

From the therapeutic standpoint, man is a passive responder whose behaviour is manipulated by the therapist. He is changed and plays no part himself in the change. He cannot plan, set himself goals, or have aims.

Dollard and Miller made man passive when they translated Freud's concepts into learning theory language. Repression for Freud was a very active affair. He said 'the essence of repression lies simply in turning something away, and keeping it at a distance, from the conscious.' (1957:147) But for Dollard and Miller it was something that resulted from the lack of verbal labels.

Both behaviour therapy (e.g. Wolpe) and behaviour modification (Skinner) are based on the findings from a number of experimental studies with animals which then resulted in the formulation of certain laws. These laws were applied to human behaviour and were shown to affect it. The behavioural therapist can remove symptoms, and his methods do not lead to an unusual rate of relapse, to secondary symptoms, or have otherwise harmful effects. Many behaviour therapists now say that the procedures they use bear no clear relationship to any learning theory – or theory of any kind. But they have techniques *that work*.

The distinction between behaviour therapy à la Wolpe and behaviour modification à la Skinner is worth maintaining because of their differing implications concerning human rights.

For instance, desensitization works, for some at least, and the procedure stems from the same view of man as does the Skinnerian model. But with desensitization the person still has *some* control over events in that he aims to control *his* gut reactions by learning to relax. One can argue that desensitizing young men to the anxiety evoked by their call-up for the Vietnam war has powerful implications concerning the rights of individuals and the State. But it would be hard to produce a reduction in anxiety by desensitization against the recipient's wish. So the main weight of the anti-behaviourist attack is against Skinner's model.

VII The rebellion

Szasz raised the issue that society can deprive an individual it deems psychologically deviant of his rights without his having recourse to law. But there is cumbersome machinery by which he can appeal to the legal process once he has been incarcerated. Now Robinson (1973) calls attention to the fact that the behaviour modifiers not only ignore or give lip-service to our rights in law, but have methods that can change our very *nature* and so could alter our *wish* to implement our rights in law. Robinson sees the *nothing-but* attitude as being largely responsible for this state of affairs. The human body is *nothing but* so much calcium, iron, and so forth. These facts are correct and yet also incorrect as a description of the living body. Such a pre-emptive construction (Kelly, 1955) saves the person the trouble of looking at other aspects of the situation and exercising judgment and is also a way of gaining control of a situation or discussion when one is not too sure of one's ground. In these senses it is scientific dishonesty.

Robinson points out that the nothing-but argument is used in the unholy alliance between neo-behaviourism and physiological psychology. With behaviourists working with the 'empty' organism and neuropsychologists with the implantation of electrodes into the brain, there was an avalanche of reported successes. 'The undeniable successes of the behaviouristic perspective led to the seemingly axiomatic conclusion that psychological man is nothing but behaviour, while data drawn from "neuropsychology" rendered psychological man nothing but a neural outcome.' (1973:130)

The alliance was predictable because both approaches had worked with the idea of man as basically a seeker after gratification – in other words, with an acknowledgement of the influence of Freud. Behaviourists work with rewards and punishments and neuropsychologists look for such things as the 'pleasure' and 'pain' centres of the brain. But for many years no one took these things too seriously, except the 'true' believers in behaviourism and neurologism. However it is one thing to condition pigeons and rats or to cut about the brains of rats and cats and quite another to contemplate their use with *us*.

But with us they are. Yet, instead of putting society on its guard against the infringement of the rights of the individual, there has grown up a belief in contingencies of reinforcement and the control of behaviour by the implantation of electrodes in the brain. 'The courts, the clinics, and the general consensus show a progressively cordial attitude toward this portrait of the New Person, and it is this attitude that determines the access science can have to the real person.' (Robinson, 1973:130)

The scientific community demands demonstrations of a procedure's validity before accepting it, but the public demands that it *works*. The therapeutic techniques of psychosurgery and behavioural engineering fall into this second category. Most behaviour therapists have long since given up the attempt to relate what they do to deductions from any learning theory and the electrode inserters have never seriously had a theoretical underpinning for their work. The techniques are employed *because they work*.

Society is faced with the possibility of transforming *psycho-*

logical man, in which case 'our right to apply these methods is bounded. It is bounded on one side by the legal force of those guarantees against cruel and *unusual* punishment and on the other side by the moral force entailed in respect for the right to be different.' (1973: 131)

A child before a juvenile court might have the possibility of two things happening to him (were he to be found guilty of an offence). He might be sent to prison or else to a special school where operant conditioning was applied to those with 'social' problems. The maximum prison sentence might be thirty days, but the conditioning procedure takes eighteen months. Robinson points out that legally it is irrelevant whether or not the child's problem has been removed. What are the child's rights in this case?

Robinson gives the story of how he attended a lecture given by an eminent neurologist. The patient demonstrated was a depressive homosexual tramp who had been revolted by a 'heterosexual' film. But, after having some electrodes permanently implanted in his brain, he not only enjoyed such films but was able to have successful sexual intercourse with a prostitute. Following the 'before and after' advertisement for implanted brain exciters, the neurologist was asked if the procedure would have been carried out if the man had been a successful depressive homosexual business man. The answer was 'no'. More conservative methods would have been used. '... the conclusion springing from this admission is that psychosurgery is adopted when the behaviour in question departs significantly from the standards of social acceptability.' (1973: 132)

In the past there has always been the theoretical possibility of anyone who feels he is being wrongfully treated having recourse to law. But that was when treatments were not notoriously successful. Now some of them are. A person can be changed in such a way that he no longer *wants* to complain. It is no good saying that it is nothing but the behaviour that has changed. Can 'I' remain the same while my behaviour

119

changes? Robinson asks whether, if society had treated Fitzgerald's alcoholism, Leonardo's homosexuality, Poe's drug abuse, and van Gogh's depression, they would have survived as the same individual *persons*.

Nothing in the present legal system gives any guidelines as to the rights of an individual in relation to these successful 'treatments'. Each therapist has to work out his own set of ethical rules. Unlike medicine, psychology has been conspicuously silent when it comes to issues of law and ethics. But if society were only aware of the dismal paucity of psychology's facts, surely laws would come speedily. Each one of us as client/patient has to rely on the ethical views of our therapist; on the extent to which he does his best to preserve our ability to judge what is in our *own best interest*, as opposed to the best interest of society.

Here is just one example of what Robinson is talking about. McConnell points out that there are liberal doctrines that say crime is society's fault and conservative ones that say all men are basically evil and the only way to stamp out crime is to punish it severely. But neither work. 'Somehow we've got to learn how to *force* people to love one another, to *force* them to want to behave properly. I speak of psychological force. Punishment must be used as precisely and as dispassionately as a surgeon's scalpel if it is to be effective.' (1970:14)

Punishment would be laws that served as negative reinforcement:

We should try to regulate human conduct by offering rewards for good behaviour whenever possible instead of threatening punishment for breaches of the law. We should reshape our society so that we all would be trained from birth to want to do what society wants us to do. We have the techniques now to do it. Only by using them can we hope to maximize human potentiality. Of course, we cannot give up punishment entirely, but we can use it sparingly ... we'd assume that a felony was clear evidence that the criminal had somehow acquired full-blown social neurosis and needed to be cured, not punished. We'd send him to a rehabilitation centre where he'd undergo positive brainwashing until we were quite sure he had become a law-abiding citizen who would not again commit an anti-social act. *We'd probably have to restructure his entire personality.* (McConnell, 1970:74)

He is aware of the tremendous moral and legal issues such methods raise but says we should not shirk from doing what is right because of difficulties. Nor should we cling to the old-fashioned belief that we own our own personalities, since these are the product of our genetic constitution and the society into which we are born. He ends as persuasively as he began:

The techniques of behavioural control make even the hydrogen bomb look like a child's toy and, of course, they can be used for good or evil. But we can no more prevent the development of this new psychological methodology than we could have prevented the development of atomic energy. By knowing what is scientifically possible and by taking a revolutionary viewpoint toward society and its problems, we can surely shape a future more sanely than we can if we hide our collective heads in the sand and pretend that it can't happen here. Today's behavioural psychologists are the architects and engineers of the Brave New World. (1970:74)

This is food for thought indeed.

7
Man-at-odds-with-himself

I Introduction

So different is the phenomenological approach from the dynamic and behaviourist that a reminder of the philosophical background is in order. The philosopher Kant described two distinct aspects of the world: the *noumena* (the essential 'thing' which is independent of our senses) and the *phenomena* (our knowledge of the 'thing' gained through our senses). It is probable that we can never know the *noumena* since everything is inevitably filtered through our senses. This means that man can only be understood through the eyes of other men. Kant also introduced the word *transcendental* to describe the ability man has to turn his attention on to himself and so study his own mind. We *transcend* when we focus on ourselves and become aware of our own activity.

II Rogers' client-centred therapy

Phenomenology in its purest form can be found in the work of Carl Rogers. For him there is no body-mind problem since these are united by a *phenomenal field* which combines all our experiences. This field '... includes all that is experienced by the organism, whether or not these experiences are consciously perceived ... only a portion of that experience, and probably a very small portion, is *consciously* experienced. Many of our sensory and visceral sensations are not symbolized.' (Rogers, 1951:483)

In Rogers' view, few men know themselves and it is impossible for anyone to know another's phenomenal field. But his theory has been called a 'self' theory since he places great importance on getting to know oneself as much as possible. The self is the conscious part of the phenomenal field. And the self concept is a series of hypotheses one has about oneself – right or wrong.

Sometimes a person is aware of an incongruence between what he is experiencing and the way in which he perceives himself. This incongruence may lead to anxiety, depression, and threat. It is the job of the therapist to create a situation in which the *client* can change himself. With Rogers we have a *client* instead of a *patient* and an *interview* instead of a *therapeutic session*. In this approach there is no diagnosing to be done since any changes that occur are those brought about by the client himself.

Rogers' psychotherapeutic method arose not from a psychological theory but directly from philosophical views concerning the nature of man. No doubt because of this the therapeutic procedure focuses on the relationship.

a) *The relationship*

It is the relationship itself that is of paramount importance in client-centred therapy. The therapist must show warmth of feeling and understanding, coupled with a non-evaluating attitude; there is no interpreting, no probing, no personal reactions. Given such a relationship (something unlike anything the client has experienced before), a process of change can occur. The relationship is non-directive, non-authoritarian, but also much more. One person in the relationship helps another person develop 'more appreciation of, more expression of, more functional use of the latent inner resources of the individual'. (Rogers, 1961:40)

One of the important aspects of this relationship is that the therapist is totally congruent. This means he does not distort what is happening between himself and his client. Another is that the therapist must always think the client of great value no matter what he may think of his client's specific acts (*unconditional positive regard*). A third requirement in the relationship is empathic understanding. This means that the therapist must have an accurate perception of what the person is thinking and feeling. These requirements of Rogers make every man a potential therapist for every other man. All of us go through a series of such relationships in life, either helping others or being helped.

He retains the notion of *insight*, regarding it as a very important aspect of change and he defines it as the perception of new meaning in the individual's own experience. Likewise, he deals with *transference* within his own system, but regards it as relatively unimportant compared with the part it plays in Freudian psychoanalysis. It is much more unlikely for childlike dependence to occur in the client-centred adult-to-adult therapeutic relationship than in the child-to-parent relationship of psychoanalysis.

b) *The model man*

Rogers' model man is clearly very different from the models discussed so far. In the following excerpt, Rogers sums up how he sees behaviourist man and Freudian man and goes on to describe his man:

For the behaviourist, man is a machine, a complicated but nonetheless understandable machine, which we can learn to manipulate with greater and greater skill until he thinks the thoughts, moves in the directions, and behaves in the ways elected for him. For the Freudian, man is an irrational

124

being, irrevocably in the grip of his past and of the product of that past, his unconscious.

It is not necessary to deny that there is truth in each of these formulations in order to recognize that there is another perspective. From the existential perspective, from within the phenomenological internal frame of reference, man does not simply have the characteristics of a machine, he is not simply a being in the grip of unconscious motives: he is a person in the process of creating himself, a person who creates meaning in life, a person who embodies a dimension of subjective freedom. He is a figure who, though he may be alone in a vastly complex universe and though he may be part and parcel of that universe and its destiny, is also able in his inner life to transcend the material universe; he is able to live dimensions of his life which are not fully or adequately contained in a description of his conditionings or of his unconscious. (1964:129)

With this phenomenological approach we are faced fairly and squarely with *you* and *I*; with what you and I make of our own personal worlds. Gone are attempts to impose on us interpretations of our behaviour from theoretical systems that are not our own. With this subjective freedom comes, of course, responsibility. Systems using notions of unconscious forces or contingencies of reinforcement suggest we need not always be seen as responsible for our actions – which can often be something of a relief. But here our fate is placed back into our own hands and, if we get into a mess, it is up to each one of us to get himself out of it. This is not to say that we can always help ourselves – we may need external help and the client-centred therapist is there to provide the psychological climate that will best suit our present needs.

c) *Groups*
Rogers has also had a good deal to say on *encounter groups*. These were started by Lewin and his associates and later

became known as T-groups or sensitivity training groups (Marrow, 1969). As these have evolved over the last decade, there has been increasing emphasis on freedom of expression, emotional growth, fulfilment of one's potential, 'feeling', and so forth. Other types of group emphasize the experiencing of oneself and of others in the group with honesty, awareness, freedom, and trust. The tremendous rise in popularity of these encounters, particularly in North America, has mostly been among people who are still functioning in a socially acceptable manner. For instance, if you feel you have not reached your full potential, such a group experience may help you find out exactly what that potential is. You can get this opportunity over a weekend, in the nude, in the swimming-pool, in a marathon setting, or by being in 'contact' day and night.

In 1970, Blanchard described the scene vividly in an article entitled 'Ecstasy without agony is baloney':

> The whole group scene has become dangerously easy to ridicule ... Growth centres compete with one another to sign up leaders with the most prestige and to billboard the most impressive-sounding seminar titles. There is a rush to invent new and different awareness enhancing techniques ... As the centres vie with one another the Workshop titles become more grandiose. William Schutz at Esalen began with a rather modest promise of 'Joy' and followed it with 'More Joy'. Herbert Otto ... introduced 'Peak Joy' when he was at the University of Utah. Then the Elysium Institute at Los Angeles countered with 'Cosmic Joy' and 'Advanced Cosmic Joy', for which the 'Awakening Seminar' is a prerequisite. Any day now we can anticipate a program on Super Advanced Cosmic Joy. Like the makers of Tide, Bold and Ivory soap, the seminarists are always improving their product. (1970:8)

He then goes on to give examples of some individuals who have been destroyed by such experiences. He considers that one of the destructive aspects of such groups is the pressure

126

to have some ecstatic or 'peak' experience and the literature encourages the belief that such experiences are not only good but *necessary* for continuing mental health – people are 'programmed for peaks'. But as Maslow has found (see D1), such experiences are relatively uncommon and are not easy to produce on demand. This can lead to feelings of failure, disillusionment, or abnormality when others are seen to be 'successful'.

The general opinion about such groups seems to be that, in the hands of experienced people, the opportunity to speak frankly about oneself and others, to behave in a relatively uninhibited way and, in the safe setting of a group, to disregard social convention, can prove beneficial to many and harmful to few. But, where people are encouraged to act at an 'awareness' level, some are going to experience deep emotional feelings and this is genuinely potentially dangerous.

Rogers is well aware of the psychological 'bomb' qualities of small groups and aims specifically to make members feel safe with each other and not threatened so that each member can truly profit from the experience. But even with an experienced person like Rogers, it is not unknown for participants to become grossly mentally disturbed and even to develop what the psychiatrist would call a psychosis.

III Kelly's personal construct therapy

Kelly's construct theory (1955) sits uneasily in this section because he was at pains to point out that his was not a phenomenological theory. It is true that for Kelly man's own interpretations of the world are of paramount importance. But other people also come into the picture. We can certainly come to understand another by observing or listening to his abstractions or constructions concerning this other's behaviour. So, to understand him, we attempt to see things as he does by placing our own constructions over his, rather than limiting ourselves to an interpretation of his overt behaviour. The more we are able to subsume another's construction of events and so look at the world as he does, the more we may hope to understand his view of that world.

But most important of all, Kelly's man has a past, a history, that can be explored, and sometimes present troubles can be seen as related to past constructions.

a) *The model man*

With a philosophical statement that 'we assume that all of our present interpretations of the universe are subject to revision or replacement', personal construct theory has built within it the seeds of its own destruction, but therein also lies each person's hope – he can change. Similarly, the statement, 'there are always some alternative constructions available to choose among in dealing with the world' (1955:15), has far-reaching implications. Gone are the problems of dualism. There is body and there is mind. Assuming that man exists, then it is equally valid to see him in physical as in mental terms. All models of man are just such alternative constructions.

Kelly's man is active. He is constantly interpreting events as seen through his unique pair of construct goggles. Kelly's model man is *man-the-scientist* in that he tries to understand his world in much the same way as the scientist in the white coat does. His behaviour can be seen as asking questions of his world in much the same way as for Galileo an experiment was a question put to nature. No motivational concepts are necessary for Kelly to explain man's quest for answers since man is alive and thus in a constant state of change.

b) *The deviant*

For Kelly psychological disorder is 'any personal construction which is used repeatedly in spite of consistent invalidation'. (1955:831) The path of change is to reconstrue for 'man is neither a prisoner of his environment nor the slave of his biography'. (1955:730)

The deviant, who is traditionally classified or diagnosed as mentally ill, is seen in construct theory terms as a scientist who is conducting unsatifactory experiments. For instance, they may not be designed to adequately answer the question being put to the test; or they are testing an hypothesis that does not logically stem from the underlying theory; or the questions or hypotheses have been formulated in such a way that it is not possible to decide whether the results support the predictions or invalidate them. In other words, the person is seen as looking at himself and at the life around him through his own unique set of theories or constructs but for some reason they are not in very good working order.

Kelly's model leads the clinical psychologist to place the other person in the centre of the picture. In a sense this is similar to Szasz's person who has a problem with living. But Kelly's approach takes one much further. One is not so much concerned with social norms and social values, as with how the individual person is interpreting and 'using' these norms and values. Kellyian man understands others by listening to what they have to say, not listening in the sense of hearing words, but listening to what the person is trying to convey. To understand another we put on *his* construct goggles and look at the world through *his* eyes. Kelly points out that if you want to know what a person's problem is – ask him, for he just might tell you.

c) *Diagnosis*

With a construct theory view of man, diagnosis takes on a very different complexion from that used in medicine. One is not concerned with fitting people into specific categories, nor with identifying conflicts, repression, denial, or specific complexes. But the complaint or symptom is a good place for the person to start. A clear picture of the complaint is of extreme importance – that is, a picture of the complaint *as the person sees it*. A person has become 'ill' because he has been unable to adapt his construct system to deal with certain vital aspects of life. He has attempted to rearrange some of his constructs and make those that govern them (the superordinate ones) less rigid in their application. When he makes a bad job of this he will develop 'symptoms'. For Kelly, a symptom is 'the rationale by which one's chaotic experiences are given a measure of structure and meaning'. (1955:366)

You may see that this has some similarity with the psychodynamic notion that people 'escape into illness'. But in this case, the therapist does not look to see what he is escaping from by delving into the past, but looks to see in what way the person's present way of looking at life is inadequate for his needs.

To help in the diagnosis the therapist uses his professional construct subsystem. He decides whether something is deviant by relating this behaviour to his own set of norms or constructs to do with that type of behaviour. The clinician starts to think something is wrong when he feels that he is unable to predict the behaviour of a person as well as he would be able to do with another similar person. His task is to find what it is in the general organization of the patient's construct system that has enabled him to 'paint himself into a corner' – he is stuck and can find no way out.

One of the professional constructs Kelly emphasizes is dependency. Kelly does not like using the trait labels of 'dependent' or 'independent' because he sees each person as being both in different areas of his life. Dependency starts in early life when we focus our attention on some figure – usually our *mother*. We are dependent on her for survival. Such a dependency construct is a figure construct and is *pre-verbal*. It is a figure construct in that it is *mother* and not father or anyone else; mother behaves in certain characteristic ways which are not to be found in anyone else who is not construed as *mother*. There are certain behaviours that come to be applied to other people as we get older, but this comes under the construct *motherliness*.

d) *Unconscious and pre-verbal construing*

The figure construct *mother* is a pre-verbal construct in the sense that it is not available to us to think about in a logical way (or an illogical way for that matter). Pre-verbal constructs are seen in a very different way from the unconscious as proposed by the psychoanalysts. There is no 'dynamic', no force, attached to them. But they can make us 'do' things in ways that seem strange and irrational to us. It is helpful perhaps to think of constructs as being essentially discriminations. They are ways in which certain elements or aspects of life are alike and thereby different from others.

If we use such dependency constructs in adulthood, we may find ourselves in trouble. For these are very impermeable. That is, 'this is mother and nothing-but mother and I expect from her specific mother-type things'. Thus in adult life a man may constantly go around seeing women as either *like mother* – in which case he predicts they are above reproach, loving, self-sacrificing, and generally nurturing – or *not like mother* – in which case they are beyond the pale because they are wicked, sexy, grasping and, worse, want him to do wicked things himself. Such a man will feel that it is not he who is wrong, but that the world is full of these wicked women and his only chance of happiness is to find another *mother*. It is often when a person is employing a dependency construct that the psychoanalyst will interpret the resulting behaviour as 'acting out'. For with a pre-verbal construct placed over events, the person can only 'behave'. It is also pre-verbal constructs that are being employed when 'transference' takes place.

Kelly considered that the child matures as he is increasingly able to make these figure dependency constructs more permeable. That is, people can be a bit like mother or a bit unlike her. It becomes an attribute. A person can be motherly in some respects and quite unmotherly in others.

Pre-verbal constructs are not role constructs, since the essential aspect of the role is the ability to see the world

131

through the other person's eyes. Role constructs develop as the child begins to understand that, just as he is construing others, so they, in turn, are construing him.

e) *The relationship*

The therapeutic relationship is essentially one in which two people struggle to understand why one is failing to solve the problems he encounters in life. Kelly likened the relationship to that between a Ph.D. student and his supervisor. The one knows a lot about the area of concern – after all he has chosen it – the other knows something about the pitfalls that the student can encounter and some of the ways to help him get out of the mess he is presently in. Both are in the task together and the patient will get nowhere if he is simply 'patient'. He must work, and work hard.

The therapy room is seen as a laboratory in the sense that it is a place where the client or patient may conduct experiments in relative safety. During the experimental sessions or interviews, the therapist must be accepting. In this sense he is similar in his behaviour to the psychoanalytic or Rogerian therapist. But it is accepting with a difference. Not only does it emphasize the patient's right to determine his own destiny, but the therapist shows the patient that he is able to interpret things the way the patient does and that, in effect, he understands the patient in a real sense. When the patient is aware of this, he feels 'supported' and able to be more adventurous. This does not mean that there is general acceptance or approval of everything the patient says or does. But just that he has an idea of how the world is looking to that patient.

A particularly important part that the therapist plays is as validator of the patient's behavioural experiments. The patient can be helped to see how effective some new ways of behaving are going to be by observing the responses of his therapist. Kelly described a specific form of interaction which he called Fixed Role Therapy in which patient and therapist can work out new roles that might help the patient in developing new behavioural experiments. The therapist might respond in different ways to show some of the alternative responses the patient might get to his new behaviours outside the therapy room. But Fixed Role Therapy is only an example Kelly gave of how his theory of personal constructs might be applied to help in the patient's task of reconstruing his world.

Kellyian man is a Kantian man and, when he has problems, the help he gets is from another *person*. The only way one person can help another in this psychological sense is for one to try and subsume the construct system of the other and, in doing so, set out alternative construct avenues the other might explore.

f) *The rebellion*
It is yet to come. Rebellion most often comes from within an established group and Kelly's model is not sufficiently well known yet for dissidents to have emerged.

IV Need to change?

Whose need are we talking about? If we follow Locke and the empiricists we, the scientists, will look at the organism – psychology. Do we see it as needing to change? Many books in *Essential Psychology* will give a negative answer. They will give the state of the discipline at this point in time and show little evidence of discontent. Others will shout loud and long that all is far from well.

But what of those as yet barely perceptible shifts that are taking place in the very foundations of psychology? That is in those jigsaw puzzle pieces which, put together, psychologists hope will resemble 'man' – learning, perception, memory, and so forth.

a) *Changing psychology and psychologists*
Bandura, one of the heavyweights in psychology, gave the Presidential Address at the 1974 meeting of the American

Psychological Association in which he said that many people equated behaviour therapy with conditioning:

> Over the years, the terms *behaviourism* and *conditioning* have come to be associated with odious imagery, including salivating dogs, puppetry, and animalistic manipulation. As a result, those who wish to disparage ideas or practices they hold in disfavour need only to label them as behaviouristic or as Pavlovian precursors of a totalitarian state. Contrary to popular belief, the fabled reflexive conditioning in humans is largely a myth. Conditioning is simply a descriptive term for learning through paired experiences, not an explanation of how the changes come about. Originally, conditioning was assumed to occur automatically. On closer examination it turned out to be cognitively mediated. People do not learn despite repetitive paired experiences unless they recognize that events are correlated ... So-called conditioned reactions are largely self-activated on the basis of learned expectancies rather than automatically evoked. The critical factor, therefore, is not that events occur together in time, but that people learn to predict them and to summon up appropriately anticipatory reactions. (Bandura, 1974:859)

But no matter what Bandura says, the conditioning concept is a mechanistic one as shown in the first chapter. No amount of tarting up will make it anything else.

Suppose we shift now to a Kantian perspective and ask ourselves whether psychologists as individuals are feeling the need to change what they do. Bandura has found the conditioning model wanting in its ability to help us understand man's complexities and so is trying to stretch it to make it a better fit. But he may find that it will part at the seams.

Also in *American Psychologist*, we find Jenkins (1974) asking 'Remember that old theory of memory? Well, forget it!' In discussing the results of a number of experiments he gives his views on what is to be learnt from them:

> I think it is clear that we should shun any notion that memory consists of a specific system that operates with one set of rules on one kind of unit. What is remembered in a given situation depends on the physical and psychological context in which the event was experienced, the knowledge and skills that the subject brings to the context, the situation in which we ask for evidence for remembering, and the relation of what the subject remembers to what the experimenter demands ... It (contextualism) suggests that we look to the subject's ways of constructing and reconstructing his experience. (1974:793)

Just two examples of the rumblings of change that are taking place well outside the realms of applied psychology. Psychologists are increasingly questioning some of their most fundamental beliefs. But if we start off with Kant's rather than Locke's perspective, then man *is* a form of action and so is *constantly* changing. How much more exciting life is when we can feel responsible for our own actions and have expectations, anticipations, and hopes for change that is yet to come than it is if we are capable only of reaction to events outside our own control.

b) *Resistance to change*

But because we may like change and regard it as an essential feature of living, it does not mean that we always welcome it. Why is it that virtually all human beings resist change on occasion? Resistance in psychotherapy is talked of a great deal, but it is seldom discussed outside that context.

One explanation can be given based upon Kelly's notion of threat. We are threatened when faced with imminent comprehensive change in our 'core' construing. Core constructs are those that give us our sense of identity. Thus, a behaviourist – that is one who has invested a great deal of himself in

135

'being' a behaviourist – might be threatened if he were to come face to face with the possibility that his scientific approach really gives him little understanding of the complexities of man. The threat would be the awareness that, if he accepted this possibility, he would have to make many other radical changes in the ways in which he carried out his daily work, viewed his past professional labours, and contemplated his possible alternative self – as one of those 'soft' humanists! Too much change in the offing and the best thing to do is retrench.

c) *The future*

Who can say? Much of this unit focuses on change and the present change is in the direction of making the person rather than his mechanics the centre of psychological inquiry.

If we continue along the path directed by Kant – the path of freedom – then this freedom of the individual to develop in his own way, to decide on his own future, will call certain aspects of psychology into question. But there are other questions. Is education a means whereby a child is moulded into the shape dictated by society or a time when a child can achieve freedom to develop in a personal sense? Is industry a place where the psychologist works for the personal development of individual workers or where he aims to ensure that workers conform to the dictates of that industry? Is the psychologist working in a mental hospital there to help pin diagnostic labels on patients or to help an individual struggle with his present failures and discover his strengths? If we are to be in the personal development business then advertising and market research are obviously outside the psychologist's purview.

The implications of the changes that are taking place in psychology today are tremendous and may well rend the discipline in two.

References
and Name Index

The numbers in italics following each entry refer to page numbers within this book.

Aristotle (1952) In R. M. Hutchins (ed.) *Great Books of the Western World, 8.* Chicago: Encyclopaedia Britannica. *10*

Ayer, A. J. (1946) *Language, Truth and Logic.* New York: Dover Publications. *18*

Balint, M. (1957) *The Doctor, his Patient and the Illness.* London: Pitman. *65*

Baloff, N. and Becker, S. W. (1967) On the futility of aggregating individual learning curves. *Psychological Reports 20*: 183–91. *53, 54*

Bandura, A. (1974) Behavior theory and the models of man. *American Psychologist 29*: 859–69. *134*

Bannister, D. (1966) A new theory of personality. In B. Foss (ed.) *New Horizons in Psychology.* Harmondsworth: Penguin. *15*

Bannister, D. (1968) The logical requirements of research into schizophrenia. *British Journal of Psychiatry 114*: 181–8. *76*

Bannister, D. and Mair, J. M. M. (1968) *The Evaluation of Personal Constructs.* London: Academic Press. *56*

Bannister, D., Salmon, Phillida and Leiberman, D. M. (1964) Diagnosis–treatment relationships in psychiatry: a statistical analysis. *British Journal of Psychiatry 110*: 726–32. *76*

Beloff, J. (1973) *Psychological Sciences.* London: Staples. *45*

Berent, P. (1966) The technique of the depth interview. *Journal of Advertising Research 6. 101*

Blanchard, W. (1970) Ecstasy without agony is baloney. *Psychology Today 3*: 8–9. *126*

Bolles, R. C. (1962) The difference between statistical hypotheses and scientific hypotheses. *Psychological Reports 11*: 639–45. *41*

Bolton, D. (1975) Two concepts of man. *Proceedings of the British Psychological Society Conference, Nottingham. 37*

Brooks, K. (1973) Freudianism is not a basis for a Marxist psychology. In P. Brown (ed.) *Radical Psychology*. London: Tavistock Publications. *30, 104*

Burtt, E. A. (1955) *The Metaphysical Foundations of Modern Physical Science*. New York: Doubleday and Co. *12*

Cook, S. W., Hicks, L. H., Kimble, G. A., McGuire, W. J., Schoggen, P. H. and Smith, M. B. (1972) Ethical standards for research with human subjects. *American Psychological Association Monitor 3*: I–XIX. *43*

Descartes, R. (1927) Letter to Henry More. In R. M. Eaton (ed.) *Descartes Selections*. New York: Scribner. *13*

Dollard, J. and Miller, N. E. (1950) *Personality and Psychotherapy: An Analysis in Terms of Learning, Thinking, and Culture*. New York: McGraw-Hill. *107, 108*

English, H. B. and English, Ava (1958) *A Comprehensive Dictionary of Psychological and Psychoanalytic Terms*. New York: Longmans. *95*

Eysenck, H. J. (1960) Classification and the problem of diagnosis. In H. J. Eysenck (ed.) *Handbook of Abnormal Psychology*. London: Sir Isaac Pitman. *88*

Freud, S. (1953) The interpretation of dreams. *The Standard Edition of the Complete Psychological Works of Sigmund Freud, IV and V*. London: Hogarth Press. *102*

Freud, S. (1957) On the history of the psychoanalytic movement, papers on metaphysical psychology, and other works. *The Standard Edition of the Complete Psychological Works of Sigmund Freud, XIV*. London: Hogarth Press. *98, 116*

Freud, S. (1961) The future of an illusion, civilization and its discontents, and other works. *The Standard Edition of the Complete Psychological Works of Sigmund Freud, XXI*. London: Hogarth Press. *103*

Freud, S. (1963) Introductory lectures on psychoanalysis. *The*

Standard Edition of the Complete Psychological Works of Sigmund Freud, XV. London: Hogarth Press. *102*

Freud, S. (1964) (trans. W. D. Robson-Scott) *The Future of an Illusion*. New York: Doubleday and Co. *105*

Goffman, E. (1968) *Asylums*. Harmondsworth: Penguin. *80, 81*

Greenspoon, J. (1954) The effect of two non-verbal stimuli on the frequency of members of two verbal response classes. *American Psychologist 9*: 384. *112*

Guertin, W. H. (1961) Medical and statistical–psychological models for research into schizophrenia. *Behavioural Science 6*: 200–4. *76*

Haley, J. (1963) *Strategies of Psychotherapy*. New York: Grune and Stratton. *96, 100*

Hampden-Turner, C. (1971) *Radical Man*. London: Duckworth. *43*

Henley, Nancy and Brown, P. (1974) The myth of skill and the class nature of professionalism. In *The Radical Therapist*. Harmondsworth: Penguin. *94*

Hull, C. L. (1937) Mind, mechanism and adaptive behaviour. *Psychological Review 44*: 1–32. *22*

Jahoda, Marie (1958) *Current Concepts of Positive Mental Health*. New York: Basic Books. *68, 71, 72*

Jahoda, Marie (1972) Social psychology and psychoanalysis: a mutual challenge. *Bulletin of the British Psychological Society 25*: 269–74. *67, 104*

Jenkins, J. (1974) Remember that old theory of memory? Well forget it! *American Psychologist 29*: 785–95. *134, 135*

Kant, I. (1902) *Metaphysische Anfangsgrunde der Naturwissenschaft*. (Akademic ed. *IV*, trans. T. Mischel) Berlin: Reimer. *27*

Kant, I. (1909) Critical examination of practical reason. In T. K. Abbot (trans.) *Critique of Practical Reason and Other Works*. New York: Longmans. *27*

Kelly, G. A. (1955) *The Psychology of Personal Constructs, 1 and 2*. New York: Norton. *31, 51, 53, 66, 95, 117, 127, 128, 130*

Kelly, G. A. (1962) Europe's matrix of decision. In M. R. Jones (ed.) *Nebraska Symposium*. University of Nebraska Press. *34*

Kelly, G. A. (1965) The strategy of psychological research. *Bulletin of the British Psychological Society 18*: 1–13. *38*

Kelly, G. A. (1966) Transcript of tape-recorded conversation with Fay Fransella. *63*

Kelly, G. A. (1969a) Humanistic methodology in psychological research. In B. Maher (ed.) *Clinical Psychology and Personality.* New York: Wiley. *24*

Kelly, G. A. (1969b) Sin and psychotherapy. In B. Maher (ed.) *Clinical Psychology and Personality.* New York: Wiley. *31*

Koch, S. (1964) Psychology and emerging conceptions of knowledge as unitary. In T. Wann (ed.) *Bahaviourism and Phenomenology.* Chicago: Univ. of Chicago Press. *17*

Kunnes, R. (1974) Detherapizing society. In *The Radical Therapist.* Harmondsworth: Penguin. *94*

Laing, R. D. (1967) *The Politics of Experience and the Bird of Paradise.* Harmondsworth: Penguin. *80*

Magee, B. (1973) *Popper.* London: Collins. *21*

Maher, B. A. (1966) *Principles of Psychotherapy.* New York: McGraw-Hill. *87*

Marrow, A. J. (1969) *The Practical Theorist: The Life and Work of Kurt Lewin.* New York: Basic Books. *126*

Maslow, A. H. (1950) *Self-actualizing People: A Study of Psychological Health.* Personality Symposia I. New York: Grune and Stratton. *70*

McConnell, J. B. (1970) Criminals can be brainwashed – now. *Psychology Today 3*: 14–18, 74. *120, 121*

Milgram, S. (1974) *Obedience to Authority.* London: Tavistock Publications. *43*

Mowrer, O. H. (1960) Sin: the lesser of two evils. *American Psychologist 15*: 301–4. *87*

Nunnally, J. (1960) The place of statistics in psychology. *Education and Psychological Measurement 20*: 641–50. *41*

Orne, M. T. (1962) On the social psychology of the psychological experiment: with particular reference to demand characteristics and their implications. *American Psychologist 17*: 776–83. *42*

Polatin, P. and Philtine, Ellen (1949) *How Psychiatry Helps.* New York: Harper. *95*

Popper, K. (1959) *The Logic of Scientific Discovery.* London: Hutchinson. *20*

Popper, K. (1972) *Conjectures and Refutations: The Growth of Scientific Knowledge.* (4th ed.) London: Routledge and Kegan Paul. *19, 20, 21, 35*

Rachman, S. (1971) *The Effects of Psychotherapy*. London: Pergamon Press. *114*

Resnick, J. H. and Schwartz, T. (1973) Ethical standards: an independent variable in psychological research. *American Psychologist 28*: 134–39. *44*

Robinson, D. N. (1973) Therapies: a clear and present danger. *American Psychologist 28*: 129–33. *117, 118, 119*

Rogers, C. R. (1951) *Client-Centered Therapy*. Boston: Houghton Mifflin. *96, 123*

Rogers, C. R. (1961) *On Becoming a Person*. Boston: Houghton Mifflin. *124*

Rogers, C. R. (1962) Some learnings from a study of psychotherapy with schizophrenics. *Pennsylvania Psychiatry Quarterly*, 3–15. *96*

Rogers, C. R. (1964) Towards a science of personality. In T. W. Wann (ed.) *Behaviourism and Phenomenology*. Chicago: Chicago University Press. *125*

Roiser, M. (1974) Asking silly questions. In N. Armistead (ed.) *Reconstructing Social Psychology*. Harmondsworth: Penguin. *47*

Rosenthal, R. (1967) Covert communication in the psychological experiment. *Psychological Bulletin 67*: 356–67. *42*

Rosenthal, R. and Jacobson, L. (1968) *Pygmalion in the Classroom*. New York: Holt, Rinehart and Winston. *51*

Russell, B. (1959) *Wisdom of the West*. Garden City, N.Y.: Doubleday. *28*

Rychlak, J. F. (1968) *A Philosophy of Science for Personality Theory*. Boston: Houghton Mifflin. *28*

Rychlak, J. F. (1973) A question posed by Skinner concerning human freedom, and an answer. *Psychotherapy: theory, research and practice 10*: 14–23. *25*

Rychlak, J. F. (1974) *Introduction to Personality and Psychotherapy*. Boston: Houghton Mifflin. *104, 109*

Shaw, D., Bloch, S. and Vickers, Ann (2 Nov. 1972) Psychiatry and the state. *New Scientist*, 258–61. *86*

Siegler, M. and Osmond, H. (1974) *Models of Madness and Models of Medicine*. New York: Macmillan. (Also *Psychology Today* (1974) *8*: 71–8.) *82, 83, 84*

Skinner, B. C. (1971) *Beyond Freedom and Dignity*. Harmondsworth: Penguin. *25, 26*

Slater, P. (1972) *Notes on INGRID '72* (Unpublished manuscript). St George's Hospital, London, S.W.17. *56*

Stampfl, T. G. and Levis, D. J. (1967) Essentials of implosive therapy: a learning-theory-based psychodynamic behavioural therapy. *Journal of Abnormal Psychology 12*: 496–503. *115*

Szasz, T. (1960) The myth of mental illness. *American Psychologist 15*: 113–18. *85, 86*

Szasz, T. (1961) *The Myth of Mental Illness: Foundations of a Theory of Personal Conduct.* London: Hoeber. *80*

Szasz, T. (1969) The crime of a commitment. *Psychology Today 2*: 55–7. *86*

Watson, J. B. (1913) Psychology as the behaviourist sees it. *Psychological Review 20*: 158–77. *16*

Watson, L. (1974) *The Romeo Error.* London: Hodder and Stoughton. *67*

Watts, A. (1973) *Psychotherapy East and West.* Harmondsworth: Penguin. *91*

Wolpe, J. (1969) *The Practice of Behaviour Therapy.* New York: Pergamon Press. *112*

Subject Index

144